C000254851

Profit Rocket

Kelly Clifford

Profit Rocket

First published in 2012 by

Ecademy Press
48 St Vincent Drive, St Albans, Herts, AL1 5SJ
info@ecademy-press.com
www.ecademy-press.com

Printed and bound by Lightning Source in the UK and USA.
Cover designed by Neil Coe.

Printed on acid-free paper from managed forests. This book
is printed on demand, so no copies will be remaindered or
pulped.

ISBN 978-1-908746-32-0

The right of Kelly Clifford to be identified as the author of
this work has been inserted in accordance with sections 77
and 78 of the Copyright Designs and Patents Act 1988.

A CIP catalogue record for this book is available from the
British Library.

All rights reserved. No part of this book may be reproduced in any material
form (including photocopying or storing in any medium by electronic
means and whether or not transiently or incidentally to some other use
of this publication) without the written permission of the copyright
holder except in accordance with the provisions of the Copyright, Design
and Patents Act 1988. Applications for the Copyright holders written
permission to reproduce any part of this publication should be addressed
to the publishers.

Copyright 2012 Kelly Clifford

Dedication

For Jon and every other person that helped make this book possible. Your love and support are greatly appreciated and I couldn't have done it without you.

I also dedicate this book to all the people who have been bold enough to go into business for themselves and who have overcome all the challenges they have faced in getting to this very point.

Contents

Introduction

Welcome to Profit Rocket. This book is about giving you the tools, insights and resources you need to prepare the 'Profit Rocket' that is your business for launch. The 10-step blueprint I provide you at the end of the book will help you to dramatically increase the profits of your business.

I have written this book to help owners who have been in their business for a while and are passionate about what they do but who have become frustrated that they have nothing really to show financially for all the effort they have put in.

These business owners may see their staff earning more than they do without the associated stress and wonder why they put themselves through it all. They lack time to focus on growing profits as they are so involved in the 'doing part' of the business. They may also be a bit scared of the numbers side as it is an area in which they lack confidence, so they tend to avoid dealing with it by making excuses and hoping that by ignoring it, it will go away.

They have reached a stage where they have had enough and want to change things. They have a real desire to take their business to the next level. They don't know where to start, however, in working with and understanding their numbers and how to grow their profits. They recognise that they need the right help to move the business forward.

Equally this book is useful for people just starting out in business to get off on the right foot and to learn from the mistakes that others may have made before them.

I am a qualified accountant with over twelve years' experience, and from working as a Finance Director in a small business, I know the areas to focus on to grow profits rapidly. It is these insights that I share with you in this book by introducing you to my Profit Accelerator Formula. I also provide you with 135 ideas for strategies that you can use in your business to help increase your profit. I take you on a journey through the book, share parts of my story and provide other relevant case studies to help make the content come alive and feel real for you.

It is my hope that you will see this book as a resource you can come back to time and time again for new ideas and inspiration. I am excited for you right now and look forward to sharing the journey with you through this book and beyond, if you feel you want my further support.

I hope what you are about to read will transform the way you look at profit forever!

CHAPTER 1

Being in business isn't always easy

Being in business isn't necessarily always easy. If it were an easy thing to do then everyone would be doing it. As business owners, we find ourselves, particularly in the early stages of a business, having to be a master juggler in that we are managing a whole host of different tasks at seemingly the same time. Not only are you concerned with the 'doing part' of providing your products and services but you find that there is a myriad of other things you need to be concerned with such as marketing, managing staff, being on top of the numbers, staying updated on the ever-changing legislation landscape and ensuring that you are on top of any red-tape burden that is imposed on your business. The list doesn't end there, but you get the idea.

I don't know about you, but I have a tendency to be my own harshest critic. I don't always see the successes I am achieving as I have focused on the next milestone to reach. It usually takes someone else to point it out, which causes me to stop and truly reflect on the progress I am making. So I want to be that someone for you who makes you stop and reflect on the successes you have had along the way.

EXERCISE

Find a quiet place where you are not disturbed by email or phone calls and spend 10-15 minutes reflecting on the past and I want you to identify five key events or successes in your business that you are proud of that make you think, 'Wow, I did that!' If you can't think of **at least five** then I bet you aren't thinking hard enough and you need to dig deeper.

CHAPTER 1

1. _____

   _____

   _____

   _____

2. _____

   _____

   _____

   _____

3. _____

   _____

   _____

   _____

4. _____

   _____

   _____

   _____

5. _____

   _____

   _____

   _____

What words would you use to describe the positive things you felt when you achieved these things?

1. _____

_____

_____

_____

2. _____

_____

_____

_____

3. _____

_____

_____

_____

4. _____

_____

_____

_____

5. _____

_____

_____

_____

Firstly, congratulations on your successes!

This is quite an important exercise so please take note as you will be embarking on new things and learning new skill-sets as your business grows. I am guessing that in many of the five successes you identified above you had no idea at the outset how you would go about achieving them. Correct? Whatever doubts you may have had at the time, you did achieve your goal and that's the key point to remember.

I want you to use these successes as positive anchors as you embrace new areas that you may not be comfortable or familiar with now. Understanding and working with numbers may be one such area. The key thing to remember is that you can do it. Your successes prove that you can do it.

So if you ever find that you are questioning your ability to do something or wobbling in your belief, come back and take five minutes to reflect on the successes you have noted here and relive in your mind how it felt and use those feelings to propel and motivate you moving forward with future projects.

Over the coming pages I am going to share parts of my business journey with you. It is my hope that by sharing this and describing how I felt while it was all happening, you may be able to relate to all or parts of it. At the time I felt that I was the only one feeling like I did, but have found since that it is actually very common and almost part of the process that we go through as individuals when transitioning from an 'employee' mind set to that of a business owner.

The key message here is that you are not alone. Many people go through it but most keep it to themselves and don't share it. They adopt a 'fake it 'til you make it' mentality which – don't get me wrong – definitely has its place at the right times, but I also think there is something to be said for the provision of realistic and grounded support.

I can honestly say that I was completely unprepared for the emotional rollercoaster I would be embarking on when I chose to leave employment – which I have known all of my working life – to set up my own business. I was soon to find myself in at the deep end.

When I set out on my business journey, to say I had rose-tinted glasses was a complete understatement. Naively I thought that as I had been doing my job for over twelve years at the time, transitioning from doing it for someone else to doing it for myself would be a breeze. Wrong!

I thought that by getting a website, online client enquiries would start flooding in miraculously and people would be queuing up to work with me. It is what I refer to now as the 'build it and they will come' mentality. Well, I built it and they didn't come! I started out with a particular business model in mind and figured that people would be happy to pay for the service at that level. What I didn't factor in is the huge role that relationships play in business.

People generally buy from people they know and trust. Well, they didn't know me so they didn't have the opportunity to know whether I was trustworthy or not. At the time I read that it takes approximately ten points of contact before a person will generally trust you enough to buy from you. Quite staggering really, so I had a huge challenge ahead.

What I also failed to factor in was that I never had to go out in any of my previous roles and generate business, so this concept was completely foreign to me. The idea of selling was also foreign to me. While employed, my pay would come in regularly and it really didn't matter whether it was a busy or quiet month at work because I would be paid irrespectively.

I didn't have a meaningful network of contacts when I started out either and didn't know then how important having that network would be in time. Now to defend myself a little bit, I did think I had a chunky bit of work lined up to kick off with, but because of circumstances beyond my control, that client work fell through at the very last minute.

So there I was, having resigned from my role as Finance Director and given up the six-figure salary that went with it to set up my new business, and the client I thought I had to kick things off with pulled the rug at the last minute. Oh no!

When the rug was pulled, as it were, I knew that my focus had to be to build a network of contacts, and fast, so I threw myself into the unfamiliar world of networking.

Now, when people hear the word 'networking', they have what I can only describe as a Marmite (or Vegemite) reaction and it's instant. They either like it or hate it. I have come to like it but didn't at the beginning – far from it, actually. What put me off most about networking at the start was that there were many people constantly trying to sell to me but few actually showed any genuine interest in what I did or whether I was actually interested in their services or not.

It struck me that most people seemed to be there to fill some gap in their life on the social front and seemed more interested in the alcohol and food being served. Very few seemed the remotest bit interested in building strong business relationships. Okay, it's probably a harsh assessment, but that's how it seemed at the time.

Also, on arriving at events when people were already there in full conversation, I found myself transported back to the school playground, trying to break into the cool crowd, waiting for an opening to be invited in. In the early days I found that I would usually get stuck talking to someone who bored me senseless and I couldn't shake him or her off. At the end of the event, I found myself thinking that it was a complete waste of time and why did I bother with it. Sound familiar?

As I had never been involved in sales before either, at the same time I undertook some sales training which adopted a relatively new approach of 'trusted adviser selling' which involves putting relationship-building first before selling. Don't get me wrong here, you still need to work out your '90-second elevator pitch' – being able to tell someone who doesn't know anything about you or your business what you do and what you are looking for in the time it takes to travel up or down in a elevator.

You want to get the core messages across as quickly and concisely as possible. Don't worry if you are not confident in this area. There are many books and other resources that you can access to help develop your perfect pitch. It's like anything, though – the more you practice the more you can see how people react to what you are saying.

You will find that some things will resonate with the listener and some won't. The key really is to watch and observe reactions and refine your pitch with elements that work and discard those that don't. It is an evolving process and networking is the perfect platform to practice and practice some more. Remember more practice makes for a better pitch!

At the start, I tried all different sorts of networking groups and even those held at different times of day. Let's just say that some were more effective than others. What I realised is that you need to identify what works best for you as an individual. There is no such thing as a 'one size fits all' approach when it comes to business networking. You need to identify the forms of networking that are likely to gain you access to the profile of client you are seeking. After trying and discarding numerous networking groups, I settled on two that felt right for me.

I will share one of those with you. It is called speed networking. Think speed dating but for business. The idea is that you sit opposite another person and you each have 90 seconds to tell the other person about your respective businesses. This is where the 90-second elevator pitch I mentioned earlier comes into its own and is a perfect place to practice, practice, and practice some more. What I love about speed networking is that it is the only form of networking I have found where you are generally guaranteed to speak to everyone in the room on a one-to-one basis. Now that can't be said for most other forms of networking.

Ninety seconds is generally enough time to assess whether it is worth picking up a conversation with someone afterwards or not, so what I do is contact those people who were of interest to me from that event and suggest a further phone call or a coffee to explore ways that we may be able to work together to help each other moving forward.

Notice the emphasis at the end of the last sentence. My approach to business networking is not to sell. I definitely don't want to be seen as a pushy salesman, which makes me inwardly roll my eyes when approached by that type at an event. I approach networking with a view to building enduring relationships with the right people over time, by spending time getting to know them, building vital trust and rapport. This means always asking the question, how can we potentially work together in ways that help and are mutually beneficial to all parties involved?

I believe that the only way to build a successful business in the long term is to focus on building trusted relationships with people so they become advocates for you and your business, and by taking a collaborative approach where all parties 'win'. Anything else creates an imbalance and will eventually be unworkable if the scales are tipped too far in favour of one party to the detriment of the other.

As you can imagine, having gone to all these networking events, I have been able to speak with a lot of business owners. I ask them about their business, the challenges they are facing or have faced and the lessons learnt. I am genuinely interested in hearing their stories as everyone is different and has a variety of experiences to share. What interests me the most is that throughout all these seemingly individual conversations, some common threads can be observed.

Some of the common messages I hear from the business owners I speak to who have reached a point where they are asking themselves, 'Is it really worth it all?' include:

- Is it worth the impact it is having on my family life?
- Is it worth the impact it is having on my health?
- Why is it that my staff are earning more than me without this burden of stress I carry with me each day?
- How am I going to meet the supplier payments next week? Tax bill? Staff wages? Rent?
- I don't seem to have enough time to do anything.
- I feel like a hamster on a wheel, running fast but actually getting nowhere.
- I can't take much more of this, something has to give and I'm scared it will be me!

When the pressures start closing in, these same people start questioning whether they are actually the problem and whether they have what it takes to be in the business. This is more common than you would think and really is a cry for help.

Frequently, business owners in this situation are trying to do everything themselves because they think that is what they have to do. They are seeking perfection in all that they do. I have definitely been guilty of this way of thinking in the past.

About six months after setting up my business, I had a real crisis of confidence. I felt a bit dejected and deflated in that all my efforts over the previous six months hadn't really yielded what I considered to be any tangible results. Sure, I was busy 'doing stuff' and having meetings but I was failing miserably in my eyes to be where I thought I should be at this point.

So I took some time out for a week from the day-to-day. It was really important for me to remove myself from the situation and reflect on the previous six months.

What I realised in giving myself this space to think and reflect was that I was being too generalist in my approach. I was trying loads of different ideas, hoping that if I cast my net wide enough then I would catch something. The problem was that I was exhausting myself trying to get everything done and spreading myself very thinly. I was trying to be everything to everyone, but ended up being nobody to no one. Sound familiar?

This led me to start questioning whether I had just wasted six months entirely, whether I was cut out for creating my own business or if, in fact, I should just give up and go back to employment. Then I thought about the prospect of being an employee again and the thought filled me with dread. I am not the sort of person that likes to wallow and I really don't like feeling rudderless and lost, as I did at that point. I wanted to get back on track as soon as I could.

What I realised at that point was that I needed to relax more about things generally and stop putting so much pressure on myself to get results, and the biggest breakthrough came when I became clear on my 'why'. It is the answer to the question, "Why am I doing this?" What is the core belief that I will build my business around and which will influence the products and services my business provides its valued clients?

The answer for me was and is: "*I believe that there is tremendous power at the intersection of entrepreneurialism and numeracy.*" Now this may not mean anything to some people and that is perfectly fine. It doesn't matter. What matters is what it means to me. You see, I believe that if a business can get the balance right between the idea or product offering and an understanding of the numbers associated with it, then it creates a truly powerful combination from which to grow.

It is this realisation that led me to write this book and to develop all the supporting resources and material that follow – if readers want further help on anything covered in the book. This 'why' statement will be the essence of all future products and services that I may launch. I don't know about you, but I find knowing this and using it as the guiding light for my business is hugely empowering.

When I became clear on my 'why' everything else started to fall into place. I became clearer on the area I wanted to focus on and the type of client I wanted to help. It enabled me to be bold enough to scrap most of what I had done with confidence, as I realised that some of my actions were down to what I thought I was *expected* to do, not necessarily what I *wanted* to do. Does that make sense? Sometimes we do things that we think others expect of us, but they don't necessarily make us happy.

So what is your 'why'?

EXERCISE

In a few sentences, try to capture the essence of 'why you are in the business you are in' and 'why you do what you do'.

_____

_____

_____

_____

_____

If there is only one message you take away from this book (but I secretly hope you gain more than one insight) then it is 'you don't have to do everything yourself'. Generally, we tend to force these expectations on ourselves. Don't be hard on yourself and recognise and celebrate your successes.

What I have learned is that it is important to always play to your strengths. If you don't think yourself strong in a particular area then you have a choice. The choice is that you can either continue as you are and face the consequences of doing this or you can seek help. It is binary. If you choose one course in this instance, then you won't get the other.

This will mean that you will need to be completely honest with yourself. You need to be able to assess what's working for you and what's not in an objective way. You definitely need to be clear on what you are trying to achieve and why you are trying to achieve a particular outcome.

This principle applies equally for minor day-to-day activities, right up to the business as a whole. Being clear on the outcome you are seeking is paramount as there are usually many different ways of approaching something to achieve a desired outcome. You may not necessarily see it yourself, but someone else might see what you don't.

The reality is that nothing in business generally goes to plan, so seeking perfection in everything you do is a somewhat pointless exercise. You need to be flexible, adaptable and know your limitations. Now, I'm not saying new skills can't be learned, quite the contrary, but the questions you need to ask yourself are: "Given what I know, what am I trying to achieve and why I want to achieve it; is this the best use of my time or could perhaps someone else do it more effectively to achieve the same or a better result?"

CHAPTER 1

Remember it is important to celebrate your successes regularly. Congratulations for being bold enough in recognising some of the limitations you may have around the numbers side of your business by picking up and reading this book!

It is my mission to ensure that you have the tools, insights and resources you need to eliminate any fear of numbers and to use what you learn here to transform the profits of your business. Sound good? Great, so let's get on with it.

CHAPTER 2

It's okay, numbers aren't scary

Did you know that up to 80% of small business owners don't have a firm grasp of the numbers? I don't know about you, but I find that alarming, given the importance of what knowing the numbers has for the survival of a business, and also from a legal perspective which requires all businesses to keep detailed and accurate financial records. It is actually an offence not to do so and could result in serious fines and even imprisonment if you don't comply with the rules.

It may sound harsh, but I want to emphasise that it is a very serious issue and, as a business owner, you have obligations when it comes to the financial side that you must meet. The buck doesn't stop with staff, service providers or anyone else. The reality is that it stops with you!

Let's dispel any illusions right now. Numbers aren't scary, mythical monsters; they can't hurt you physically but they do have tremendous power when harnessed properly. The numbers side of a business is one of the most important elements of any successful business venture, however, and if ignored it is important to recognise and acknowledge that there will be consequences.

Some of the common reasons and excuses I hear from the many business owners I speak to at networking and other events are:

- I am not a numbers person
- I hate numbers
- I don't understand numbers
- Numbers are boring
- My accountant takes care of that
- I am too busy with other things
- I'm overwhelmed; I have no idea where to start with them

Let's deal with each one individually.

I am not a numbers person

It is true that we are all different and so therefore are naturally good at different things. Some of us are more creative, some more technical and some more mechanical than others. Just because we don't perceive ourselves to be good in an area doesn't mean that we can't learn more about it if it is important to us.

You see, many use these reasons, and many of the others we will discuss, as a way to deflect responsibility and divert attention from the issue. It is a way of blaming and rationalising the reasons why they aren't doing what they know they should be doing. It is a way of avoiding taking responsibility for their actions.

Do you remember when you first learned to ride a bike? Did you know how to ride it before you hopped on it? Could you just hop on that bike and set off with confidence? I suspect not. I know I couldn't. It was a foreign concept to you but you knew that you wanted to learn how to do it and were determined to do so. There is no difference between that experience and learning more about the numbers side of your business. It all comes down to your desire and willingness to take action.

You started out with a desire and willingness to learn how to ride a bike so you got someone to teach you. You started off with training wheels to build your co-ordination skills in pedalling and steering, and as your confidence grew, you reached the stage where you wanted to do it without the training wheels. The big day arrives, the training wheels are removed, and you are sitting there on the bike in anticipation of what is to come. You are not scared but brimming with confidence because it is something you know you can do. You set off and then the wobbles start, you are so focused on trying to stay upright that you forget about the steering, so off you veer into the nearby bush.

Your ego might be a bit bruised and you might have a few scratches to show for it but it's okay, because there is no real harm done. You simply pick yourself up, dust yourself off and try again. You keep trying until you become confident in riding that bike. You feel a tremendous sense of pride and accomplishment when that happens.

You see, there is no difference between learning to ride a bike and learning about the numbers side of your business. It all comes down to a desire to learn. You need to start somewhere and get help from the many resources available to take you through the training wheel stage through to the confident cycling stage. We can't expect to be good at something instantly, and as with any new skill we need to practice and practice some more. That is the only way we will get good at something.

I hate numbers

Is this really true? Ask yourself why you think you hate numbers. Dig deep to find out the real reasons. Perhaps it may be the case that you haven't been shown what's important and what's not. Perhaps there is an area where you know there are issues but you are too scared to open that can of worms for fear of what you may discover.

Let's take the emotion out of the picture for a minute. On a purely rational level, why would you hate something that is so important for the success of your business? Do you not want your business to be a huge success? Why wouldn't you be doing everything you can to make this happen? If learning more about a new area meant more profit in your pocket, would you still hate it?

I'm not saying that you have to absolutely love numbers but you need to at least have a healthy respect for them. Ignoring the numbers side of a business is akin to abusing and disrespecting the future potential of a business.

Just like a child needs nurturing to grow and reach their full potential, so does a business.

I don't understand numbers

Most people didn't know how to ride a bike before they were shown how, as I mentioned earlier in this chapter. It is exactly the same with numbers. When you were at school, you probably didn't know much about a new subject when you started it, but as the term and year progressed you learned more, became more confident in your knowledge and continued to expand your knowledge bank on that subject matter.

Learning more about numbers is an evolving process. It will take time and energy. Don't expect to be an expert on day one. The reality is that you won't be. However, you have to start somewhere as you did when you first entered the classroom as a child. Remember, evolution not revolution.

Numbers are boring

Okay, I will admit that numbers aren't necessarily everyone's cup of tea. Some people are naturally more inclined to be stronger on the numbers front than others but you need to ask yourself whether this view is just another excuse to justify not doing something about your numbers.

Just because you perceive something to be boring is absolutely no reason not to do it. View it as a necessary evil if you need to. View it any way you want to, but at the end of the day you need to deal with it.

Let me pose a question. If you take the view that numbers are boring and, given that being on top of the numbers is such an important ingredient in the ultimate success of a business, aren't you by extension taking the view that your business is boring? And if this is true, then why are you in that business at all if you are bored?

The reality is that working with and understanding the numbers side of your business is as important as the business model itself. If the desire is for a business to reach its full potential and prosper in the longer term, then you can't separate the two elements. They are one and the same.

My accountant takes care of that

This is a good one and I hear it often. But I would raise a counter argument. Is your accountant really 'taking care of it' or are you just abdicating your responsibilities so you have someone else to blame if it all goes terribly wrong?

Typically accountants are used to prepare annual statutory accounts and submit various tax and other returns. The emphasis of their involvement is usually towards historical or past information. They report on the past but not always on a timely basis. It could be three months or more after a period ends before any information is provided.

What many business owners do once the accountant has sent through the numbers for a period to them is absolutely nothing! Many don't even look at them. The email goes into the accounts folder or 'too hard' box or the reports are printed out and then binned. It is such a wasted opportunity.

Accountancy firms tend to have a portfolio of clients so I would guarantee that your business isn't as important to them as yours is to you. Would that be a fair comment? They have many clients to look after in their portfolio, of which you are just one business. Whilst you devote 100% to your business they can only devote a fraction of their time to it, so you can see that both parties have different priorities, coming at it from different angles.

You went into business for a reason so why would you then turn around and leave an area of such vital importance to someone who isn't as passionate about what you do as you are? It doesn't make sense. Don't misunderstand this point; I am not saying for one minute that you need to produce the information yourself. Your accountant or team, whether in-house or outsourced, can do the number crunching for you, but you need to be receiving timely information on the areas that matter so that you have what is needed to manage the business, to help ensure that it reaches its full potential.

If there is a problem in a particular area then you want it flagged as a potential issue very early on so you can take corrective action to avoid a bigger issue down the road. Without this timely management information on the numbers, you truly are working blind and the business will be like a rudderless ship. That rudderless ship could be heading straight towards a group of menacing looking rocks that could cause real damage.

I am too busy with other things

We are all busy, but the reality is that we all have the same amount of hours in a day. It is how we choose to spend the time we have that is important. We make decisions every day about what we deem important for our business and us. This excuse either highlights that you are doing too much yourself and need to get in additional resources to help ease the load or, more worryingly, that you don't consider the numbers side of your business important enough to focus your time and energies on.

An important but necessary distinction needs to be made between 'working in' and 'working on' a business. 'Working in' roughly translates to the 'doing part' of the business, i.e. the delivery of the products or services to your customers or clients, whereas 'working on' the business means focusing on activities and strategies to help move the business forward to its ultimate intended destination.

Does that make sense? It is the difference between operations and strategy. When it comes to eating and our diet, we are told that everything should be consumed in moderation. The exact same principle applies here. The scales need to be kept balanced. If the scales are tipped too far in favour of one side then the other side suffers.

I'm overwhelmed. I have no idea where to start with them

It's okay to feel overwhelmed at the start of something new; it is a normal and common reaction to change. What's important is that you have recognised your present limitations in this area, have a burning desire to improve them and want to take your business to the next level.

It is worth stopping and congratulating yourself on recognising how you are feeling. You are already ahead of the game compared to most other business owners out there who are still making the excuses highlighted earlier. The key to anything is to take it at your own pace and one step at a time. Remember, the key is evolution not revolution. This means that as long as you are moving forward continuously by improving your understanding and applying it, then that is enough.

When you look up at the stars at night you see billions of them and can be easily overwhelmed by their sheer numbers. If somebody asks you to point out a specific constellation, would you know where precisely to look? I suspect not. But if someone showed you where to look and what to focus on, would that make it easier? It most certainly would.

The same principle applies to the financial side of your business. It is very easy to feel overwhelmed by the volume and complexity of information in circulation, but all that volume doesn't really matter. The focus needs to be on getting help from the right resources that will show you what to focus on and, as your knowledge and experience grows, so too will your confidence.

That is precisely why I am writing this book. I want to provide you with the telescope and show you exactly where to look to see the 'profit' constellation in the stars. Now this book can't cover everything, but it can start the process by helping you to understand the five key areas you should be focusing on to accelerate the profit growth of your business. Focus on the right detail and the rest will naturally follow. Would that be helpful for you?

I have lost count of how many times I have heard excuses spouted to me when speaking with business owners as I do. But rather than being put off, I actually get excited for the person who I am speaking to. The reason I get excited is that the fundamental truth is usually that their business is generally managing to survive, albeit limping along wounded, despite the excuses.

This indicates to me that the business model is potentially a good sustainable one. The excitement comes from knowing how much stronger and better the business could be performing when the other essential ingredient of knowing and being on top of the numbers is introduced. What a tremendous opportunity that business owner has! Now that is the really exciting prospect for me and is why I do what I do.

The classic reaction by business owners who are reeling off all the excuses they can to justify why they do what they do is to demonstrate an ostrich mentality. They have their head firmly wedged in the sand, ignoring the financial reality of their business. The problem with this approach is that it doesn't achieve anything. Sure it may make you feel better in the short term, but it does nothing to improve things. It generally makes the situation worse and could ultimately prove fatal for the business as a whole if left for too long.

What are you saying?

It is time for a bit of honest self-reflection. Listen to what you are saying to others about the numbers side of the business. Are you using any of the excuses that I have mentioned?

Once you start being tuned in to the messages you are sending, the next thing to ask yourself is whether they are really true or not. This will require complete honesty. It's okay if you are making excuses; the point, though, is to recognise that you are making excuses. If you can't be honest with yourself then who can you be honest with?

So now you are standing at an intersection. You have to make a choice. There are only two paths in front of you. On the signs in front of you, the one to the left reads 'doing what you've always done' and the other 'evolution not revolution'. The first path represents your choice to continue making excuses for not embracing the numbers side of your business. It represents doing what you have always done and getting the same results, good or bad.

What you don't know at this point is that this path is circular and may eventually lead you back to this very intersection. I say 'may' because there is no guarantee that your business will survive if the financial side continues to be neglected.

The other path involves you seeking help and having the real desire to improve your understanding on the numbers front. It represents uncharted territory for you at this point, but you know that you have done things in the past that you didn't know how to do at the outset. You soon learned, though, and became better and better at it as you practised your new skill and your confidence grew. Much like when you learned how to ride a bike, to swim or ride a horse.

Now, let's not dress it up to be anything it's not. You have to choose between continuing to make excuses or facing up to the challenge head on and moving forward from here. I can't make that decision for you, no one other than you can make that decision.

Remember the whole numbers area for your business is a skill set that can be learned just like any other skill and there's absolutely nothing to be scared about. However, there are some common mistakes that owners make when managing the financial side of their business which we will explore in the next chapter. The aim is to help prevent you from making the same mistakes yourself.

CHAPTER 3

Seven common
mistakes and tips
to avoid them

In this chapter we will explore seven common mistakes many owners make when it comes to managing the financial side of their business. Some commentary will be provided around each mistake together with tips to help prevent you from making the same mistake in your business.

There will be terms and references that perhaps aren't familiar to you and further discussion on the specifics is beyond the scope of this book, so if there is anything that you don't understand, simply make a note of it and take action to find out more about it later. I will touch on this point again at the end of the chapter. There is no reason to feel overwhelmed. Remember, it is a learning process. Evolution not revolution!

Common Mistake 1 - Failing to factor in fixed costs when pricing

When deciding on pricing, many business owners make the mistake of only focusing on the gross profit margin and tend to forget about allocating something for their overheads or fixed costs. They then wonder why they don't make any profit.

There are generally two types of costs: variable costs and fixed costs.

Variable costs are those costs that tend to fluctuate with the level of sales. They include such things as direct labour, raw materials, sales commissions and delivery expenses.

Fixed costs are those costs that do not tend to fluctuate with the level of sales. They include rent, equipment leases, insurance, interest on borrowed funds and administrative salaries.

We cover the area of gross profit and net profit in a lot of detail in Chapter 5, so if this doesn't make sense now don't worry, as hopefully it will make more sense to you when you get to that part of the book.

Michael and Susan run a retail business. They sell one core product and provide a support service with it for their clients. They are passionate about their business but can't understand why, despite having a healthy 30% gross profit margin, at the end of each year they are still making a loss.

Michael and Susan buy their product wholesale for $700 and sell it for $1,000. This means that they are making $300 gross profit per sale. In their minds, if they sell 100 products they should be making $30,000 ($300 x 100) profit. What Michael and Susan haven't factored in are the overheads for running their business. The overheads or fixed costs of running their business are $100,000 per year, which includes their rent, administrative salaries, insurance, utilities, stationery, training and marketing.

When we sat down and worked through the numbers it showed that they would have to make 334 product sales each year just to break even and cover the overhead costs of their business. As soon as they made more than 334 product sales, the business would start making a net profit which is the type of profit that counts at the end of the day. This was worked out by dividing the $100,000 fixed costs of the business by the gross profit of $300 per sale ($100,000 / $300).

Michael and Susan had never done this exercise before and felt empowered by the fact that they now knew the amount of sales they needed to make so that they could begin making a decent profit from their business.

Tip

To ensure that your business is pricing profitably, it is key that the break-even point, whether it be expressed in revenue or volume, is known and understood. Break-even analysis takes into consideration all three elements of price, variable costs and fixed costs.

Common Mistake 2 – Thinking as long as money is flowing into the business bank account they are making money

Just because money is flowing into the business bank account doesn't necessarily mean that a profit is being made on it.

Many businesses fail to look at all the factors when agreeing to do work at a given price level. Usually the price is set by market forces but many business owners fail to even do a basic analysis to work out whether they can deliver the service at a cost, less the revenue received, whilst generating a sufficient profit margin above all costs – both fixed and variable.

Craig runs a lawn-mowing business. He enjoys the outdoors and the clients he has. Craig thinks that everything is okay because he is able to pay his bills on time. He gets a shock at the end of the financial year when his accountant tells him that he has made a loss. You see, Craig never sat down and worked out what price he should be charging to ensure that he makes a decent profit and he hasn't altered his prices for over five years.

Business this year was down for Craig on previous years. The higher cash flow in previous years masked the fact that Craig had really slim profit margins so therefore little room for error. A downturn in business hit him hard but was the wake-up call he needed to look at his prices more closely. After completing a pricing review, he notified his clients of the new pricing structure and was really surprised that very few of his clients decided to go elsewhere and were largely supportive. They knew that Craig provided them with a great service and they could depend on him. Craig started making more profit than ever before.

Tip

Use a top-down approach when assessing a product or service offering. This starts by taking what the market will pay for the product or service and then deducting from it the desired profit margin. You then need to determine if you can deliver the product or service at a **total cost** equal to or less than this result. If you can, then it is a green light to proceed. If you can't then you may need to look at other ways to deliver it more efficiently, reduce the desired profit margin or simply not proceed with the opportunity at all. This area is covered in further detail in Chapter 5.

Common Mistake 3 – Thinking it is job done once a client has been invoiced

It is not the end of the story when an invoice is sent to a client for payment. A business must ensure that the payment is collected in accordance with its payment terms.

There is no point in invoicing a client if payment is not collected for it. Remember, a profit isn't actually earned until the amount for the invoice is physically received as cash in the business bank account.

A business must be proactive in the collection of its invoices.

Mary runs a consulting business. She is very busy and has a full workload but is experiencing a cash flow squeeze and can't understand why. The problem is that she is so focused on the 'doing part' of her business that she has dropped the ball on chasing payment of outstanding invoices. Mary's standard payment terms are 30 days, but closer examination revealed that some invoices had been outstanding for in excess of 90 days.

Mary undertook a huge drive to collect on all overdue invoices and ensured that she had a system of reminders in place to ensure that she stayed on top of the collection of invoice payments to avoid a similar situation occurring again.

Tip

A common metric for assessing how good your business is at collecting payments for its invoices is called Debtor Days Outstanding. This metric is used to show the number of days that have elapsed between the invoice date when it was produced and the present date if payment still remains outstanding. The closer the Debtor Days Outstanding calculation is to your payment terms (e.g. 30 days is common) the better your business is at collecting payment for its invoices.

Common Mistake 4 – Not paying close enough attention to cash flow

In business, cash is king! In some ways, managing cash flow is the most important aspect of running a business. If at any time a business fails to pay an obligation when it is due because of the lack of cash, the business is technically insolvent.

Insolvency is the primary reason firms go bankrupt. Obviously, the prospect of such a dire consequence should compel businesses to manage their cash with care. Moreover, efficient cash management means more than just preventing bankruptcy. It improves the profitability and reduces the risk to which the business is exposed.

Businesses suffering from cash flow problems have no margin of safety in case of unanticipated expenses. They may also experience trouble in finding the funds for innovation or expansion. Finally, poor cash flow makes it difficult to hire and retain good employees.

Janine is the owner-manager of a specialist service company. She has never really paid close attention to her cash flow. She never thought she had to, as there has always been enough cash to pay her bills on time up to this point. She received a phone call from one of her major clients saying that they were experiencing some cash flow difficulties and needed an extension on their standard terms by at least 30 days, but it could be longer.

Janine suddenly became worried as she had a tax bill looming and also her staff monthly payroll was rapidly approaching. The thought of letting her staff down made her feel really sick. She wanted to try and avoid the time and expense of using invoice discounting or factoring and other credit facilities if she could get through this tricky period.

We sat down and produced a simple spreadsheet that enabled Janine to input and track all of her anticipated daily cash receipts and outgoings. Janine was surprised to find that delaying payment of some outgoings, and also increasing efforts to collect other monies owed had a dramatic impact on her bank balance. Janine successfully navigated the cash flow squeeze because of this close attention. Her staff and the taxman were happy as they got paid on time. This was the wake-up call that Janine needed to lift her game on the numbers side of her business. She never wanted to find herself in this position again.

Tip 🐊

The key to successful cash management lies in:

- Making realistic projections of cash-needs, including timings
- Monitoring collections and disbursements
- Establishing effective billing and collection measures
- Sticking to a budget – not overspending

Common Mistake 5 – Not producing and reviewing financial reports regularly

Many business owners I talk to have an ostrich mentality when it comes to the numbers side of their business, as we covered in the previous chapter. They just hope that everything will be fine.

When I ask these same business owners when they last spoke to their accountant, or where the last set of financial statements are, many reply that they only speak to their accountant at year-end time or respond with, "What set of financial statements?" or "In the bin."

I find these situations really alarming because apart from the legal obligations when it comes to record keeping, the business could be at serious risk because of this avoidance mentality. Numbers aren't to be feared. If working with and understanding numbers isn't a strong skill set of a business owner then they should seek help immediately.

Stephanie and Charlie run an established marketing company. They are passionate about what they do but have neglected the financial side of their business as they have been so focused on doing whatever it takes to generate new custom over the previous year to grow their business. They buy what they need when they need it and sometimes buy more than they need or duplicate purchases because of broken communication between departments.

Stephanie and Charlie get a huge shock at the end of the financial year when their accountant reveals that they have made a massive loss. They can't understand why because they have won loads of new business over the last year. You see, by not producing and reviewing expenditure and other financial reports regularly, they had no sense of how all those seemingly harmless individual purchases were mounting up. They were gobsmacked by how much they had been spending on certain areas. This was their wake-up call. Their business wouldn't survive if it had another year like this so they started producing monthly reports to track what they were spending their money on and monitoring it much more closely.

Tip

You really need to have a handle on the numbers, whether you do it yourself or enlist the help of an expert, because knowing and understanding the numbers is key to long-term business success. Management accounts should be prepared and reviewed each quarter as an absolute minimum, with a preference for monthly accounts.

Common Mistake 6 – Not having a budget

A budget is a comprehensive plan that estimates the likely expenditure and income for a business over a specific period, typically on twelve-month cycles. It is a financial road map for a business that is derived from an underlying business plan.

Budgeting describes the overall process of preparing and using a budget. A budget is a hugely valuable tool for planning and controlling finances. The process itself helps a business to determine the most efficient and effective strategies for making money and expanding its asset base.

To be successful, budgets should be SMART which means specific, measurable, achievable, realistic and timed. The SMART principle is covered in more detail in Chapter 5.

At the same time, Stephanie and Charlie sat down and worked out a twelve-month budget, which detailed how much they anticipated spending for each type of expenditure in their business together with the anticipated revenue to be generated over the next year. The exercise really made them think about what was the best use of their resources to achieve the desired outcome of a $200,000 net profit.

They could see that if they didn't track and monitor actual activity against the amount budgeted, they risked overspending in that area or undershooting on their revenue target. Either of these would put their end of year profit target in jeopardy. Each month they compared the actual results against the budget. They found that by doing this they were able to take corrective action sooner and also found that they were much more conscious of what they were spending their money on before they spent it.

Tip 🐟

A budget is a key business tool and should be prepared annually at a minimum and then chunked down into monthly and quarterly targets. Performance against budget should be actively monitored throughout the budget period, also on a monthly or quarterly basis. Unless a business tracks its actual results against the budgeted results it has no way of knowing whether it is on track to achieve its annual targets or not.

Common Mistake 7 – Wasting money unnecessarily

I guarantee that almost every business is wasting money on something unnecessarily, whether it is through paying more than they should be, buying the wrong type of input or buying things that the business doesn't actually need.

Take business utilities for instance. Most businesses simply accept what the utility companies offer them in terms of tariff. They don't know if it is even the right tariff and usually get locked into a higher tariff than is needed. I would advocate using one of the free impartial utility management services to manage this side of a business. I would advocate the same approach when it comes to office stationery and procurement.

Producing regular financial statements and having a handle on the numbers is key to effective cost management. Unless a business knows exactly what it is spending its money on, it is difficult to know where and how improvements can be made.

You will recall that Stephanie and Charlie were overspending massively before implementing the changes described. In order to help get their business back on the path to profitability, they undertook a massive cost review, which saw them look at every single expenditure type in their business. They were really surprised to find that they were able to achieve cost savings of up to 40% in some areas simply by shopping around and by negotiating better terms through buying smarter. They felt really empowered by this and back in control of their business. They were confident and excited about the future for their business again.

> **Tip**
>
> It is imperative to review your supplier terms regularly to ensure that what is being paid is competitive. Be sure to shop around for the best deal, be clear on why something is being purchased and take advantage of early payment discounts if available and cash flow permits.

Now, I am sure there are areas raised in this section that you are a bit confused about at the moment. You are also probably looking for a solution or resource to help you understand more about what we have covered and help prevent making the same mistakes yourself. That is why I have created a resource toolkit specifically to help and support you and it is designed to address all the issues raised in this chapter. Specific details of the toolkit can be found at the end of this book.

This comprehensive toolkit contains seven modules including video content, a comprehensive workbook with case studies and worked solutions, plus various tools and templates to help you in your business. This toolkit enables you to learn and understand these areas from the comfort of your own home or office without fear of feeling embarrassed or being judged by others. It's a resource you can refer back to time and time again.

The key for you is to not feel overwhelmed by anything we have covered so far. There is absolutely no reason for you to feel that way. Nobody is expecting you to know everything about everything so don't put any unnecessary pressure on yourself. If what we have covered here doesn't make sense to you now, don't worry; it will make more sense to you in time.

Your job right now is to keep learning and implementing what you learn, which is very important as we move towards exploring the main part of this book. For the time being, I want you to focus your energies on that. The purpose of this chapter is to make you aware that there will be other areas in managing the financial side of your business with which you will need to become more familiar and confident in time. But for now we are taking baby steps; remember, one step at a time, in a forward moving direction. That's what making positive progress is all about.

CHAPTER 4

Head trash around money

We all have a belief system that is individual and unique to us. It shapes our take on the world and all the various components that make it up. Our belief system is a collection of thoughts and ideas that we believe to be true which have been accumulated through what we have been told, taught and experienced during our lives.

Our belief systems are made up of lots of different individual beliefs. These can be broken down further into those that work for us and those that work against us. Behaviours and beliefs that work against us are what I call 'head trash'. Others may refer to it as 'mind chatter'.

Our belief systems impact and shape every area of our lives and encompass relationships, friendships and money. The area that we are going to focus on in this chapter is money and the relevance of it for making more profit in your business. Our internal belief system has an influence on how we react and approach any given situation and that includes money. Some beliefs we are fully aware of but others we are not, as they are unconscious and stem from our formative childhood years.

It was a widely-held belief that the world was flat until it was proven otherwise. Similarly, it was believed that Earth was the only planet in the universe until other planets were discovered. If we believe that jellybeans are the elixir for eternal youth and can cure all medical ailments, then this belief is true to us as an individual, even though it may be flawed or not strictly true.

For example, a positive belief may be that you believe in your ability to ride a bike. This positive belief comes from a culmination of the previous experiences you have had in successfully riding a bike. A negative belief may be that money is bad. Now you may have no physical proof of this belief or experience of it, but it may come from things you heard as a child that have shaped your view of money. Can you see that having a view of money as bad contradicts the objective of your business in making profit? Your belief system in this instance is working against you and what you want to achieve.

It could be leading to self-sabotage type behaviour that you are not even aware of, such as blaming others for your current circumstances, not charging what your product or service is worth, not charging for something you should be charging for, believing that you are only this or your business is only that.

You can adopt one of two approaches to building a business, attracting clients or making money. The first is an outside-in approach and the second is an inside-out approach.

Outside-in approach

The outside-in approach operates from a place of fear, lack and need. This approach holds people back from creating the businesses they would really love for themselves.

People in this state are usually seeking validation, confidence and even love from external sources. By external sources I mean from other people or things such as money, achievement of future goals – anything that doesn't originate from them as an individual.

The theory is that layers of thought cover up our natural wellbeing and that real freedom and success, which includes financial freedom, must come from the inside and a place of acceptance of who we are now.

Typical responses when this approach is adopted include:

- I will be happy WHEN I make X in income
- I can't enjoy the lifestyle I really want UNTIL I make enough money to do so
- Information-seeking approach – constantly striving for more and more information but never applying it because it doesn't come from inside
- Not being able or willing to invest in self BEFORE you 'have' the money

You see, it is contingent on some external event happening which, if that event doesn't happen, can be turned into an excuse or reason why you didn't do what you set out to do. It gives you a reason to blame others or events because that condition wasn't met.

Inside-out approach

The inside-out approach operates from a place of inner wellbeing. It is the reverse of the outside-in approach which relies on other things to happen for us to be happy, which by extension means for other people to do things for our businesses to be successful.

The types of questions you would ask yourself if adopting an inside-out approach include:

- What would I want to do in my business if I were already happy and financially free? Think of it like this: the worst-case scenario will be you have fun doing the things you love. However, the best-case scenario will be that you do what you love and make loads of money
- What income would I love to make? Note the

distinction from 'need to make' or 'think I can realistically make'

- There are no rules about how we should run our businesses – what would be some really fun ways to reach clients I want to work with and make more money?

You may have heard about the power of thought. It is based on the principle that letting your thoughts settle, and seeing thought for what it is makes space to be creative and allows insights to happen. You might have a view on this whole area. You might think it wishy-washy and airy-fairy stuff and that's okay. The point of including this section in the book is to highlight that it is almost guaranteed there will be curve balls impacting your business that aren't originating from others; they are coming from within you.

The key is to be aware of what is influencing your responses and decisions within a certain set of circumstances. If your natural response is one that works for you and your business, then great. On the other hand, if it is one that works against what you are wanting to achieve, don't you think that being aware of it so you can factor it in would be a worthwhile thing to do, especially if not doing so would be an obstacle to business success?

We were born largely a blank sheet of paper. Our beliefs and attitudes didn't exist at that point. Our minds were pure, if you like. Our attitudes and beliefs were shaped in time from the things we heard, the experiences we encountered and from what happened in the environment around us. We didn't consciously know what we were taking in, we were just taking everything in.

Now if we heard the same message more frequently than we

were hearing others then we started to believe it to be true. For example, if throughout your childhood you heard the message that money is bad and this was reinforced time and time again, then obviously you are going to think that it is true, even if it is not.

The challenge is to reverse or be able to manage the traditional outside-in view to an inside-out one. I am not saying it is an easy process. It's not. If it helps, let me share one of the areas I struggle with to this day with learnt behaviour from my childhood.

Growing up, I had one parent who was more inclined to spend money and the other who was very inclined to save money – read 'not spend' money. The dominant behaviour was one to save rather than spend. As such, a 'savings' mindset developed in me as I grew up. Some would say that isn't necessarily a bad thing, but it can be an obstacle and, like anything, a balance is needed.

You see, I find it very easy to rationalise not spending money on something even if it is something I want or need. I can talk myself out of buying something or turn it around by saying I will buy it WHEN such and such happens. Notice the 'when' in that last sentence. Instead of taking it from a place of what will make me happy, you will recognise the outside-in approach in that I am making the outcome contingent on something else happening. That way if it doesn't happen, then I have my justification for not spending the money. Do you see the distinction?

Now I know that this is my natural tendency. Being aware of it means I can recognise when it is happening. It is at that point I am faced with a choice. It is a fork in the road. The difference is that any choice I make at this point is a conscious one. It comes from being aware of my likely default behaviour. I can make a conscious decision about how to move forward with that thing in mind.

Over the years, I have surrounded myself with people and things that help me strike more of a balance when it comes to this behaviour. My partner, who is more inclined to spend than save, plays a big part in that. We help balance each other and that is the key to overcoming any limiting behaviour. The good news is that it does get easier to recognise the signs when old learnt, limiting behaviour raises its ugly head.

Uncovering your head trash around money

Having unconscious head trash when it comes to money can show itself in many ways, such as:

- Feeling guilty about making money
- Being scared to charge beyond a certain level of comfort
- Believing money is evil
- That you believe you **need** money to be happy (but you shouldn't be greedy and want too much of it)
- The more money you earn, the more important your job or role within a business is, the more important you are
- The more you earn, the more you have to sacrifice
- Time is money (we should be paid for our time – as opposed to our knowledge and expertise and value we provide)
- If we love what we do, we feel guilty about getting paid for it
- People will think we are greedy or arrogant to charge high fees
- Fear money mindset – doing something you wouldn't

normally consider out of fear of losing money.
- Desperate money mindset – being desperate for a sale
- Money corrupts
- There is not enough money to go round
- I don't want to make money because I'm scared I will lose it

What we need to do is nurture and encourage a mindset needed for success. Not one person on this planet is perfect. We all have issues or legacy emotions from past events that have shaped our behaviour, in many instances without us consciously knowing or being aware of it.

Trying to build a successful business when you have a poor, or even dysfunctional, relationship with money is like trying to drive a car with one foot on the accelerator and the other on the brake. It uses up a lot of energy and resources but doesn't get you very far.

A really great resource that I have used that delves much deeper into this area is Paul McKenna's number one bestseller *I Can Make You Rich* which I highly recommend as an excellent read on this area.

He suggests the following exercise in his book for identifying any beliefs you have around money that are working against you and sabotaging your success.

Exercise: Uncovering your money beliefs

1. Complete these twelve sentences about money, wealth and riches to uncover the key elements of your current unconscious programming:

   1. People with money are _____
      _____

   2. Money makes people _____
      _____

   3. I'd have more money if _____
      _____

   4. My parents always thought money would _____
      _____

   5. Money causes _____
      _____

   6. I'm afraid that if I had more money I would _____
      _____

   7. Money is _____
      _____

   8. In order to have more money, I would need to ____
      _____

   9. I think money _____
      _____

  10. If I were really rich, I would _____
      _____

  11. My biggest fear about money is _____
      _____

  12. Money is _____
      _____

2. Circle any of your unconscious beliefs about money that might be holding you back, even if they seem unquestionably 'true' to you.

3. Repeat this exercise daily for at least the next week. You may find some other deeper-rooted beliefs take a bit longer to come to the surface.

The shovel exercise

1. Make a list of the most negative-seeming beliefs about money you uncovered in the previous exercise.

2. Substitute the word 'shovel' (another practical tool) for 'money' in each of the sentences on your list. Notice whether the statements still make sense or have any emotional significance.

Examples

'The love of shovels is the root of all evil'
'Shovels don't grow on trees'
'I feel guilty because I have more shovels than my parents ever did'

Remember, the idea here is simply to take away the emotional 'sting' from these ideas. It doesn't matter whether or not you really believe them.

Right at the start of the book I talked about how being in business isn't necessarily always easy. There are many curve balls that are thrown at us, which we need to dodge and avoid being hit by. The key is to be able to avoid more of these curve balls than not. This means that we need to pre-empt or head off issues before they become bigger issues.

One such area that we need to be aware of is our own internal money head trash. Challenges aren't always external. We need to look within ourselves and identify anything we are doing or saying to ourselves that may be holding us back from meeting our aspirations of building a highly profitable and successful business.

Remember, some of your beliefs work for you and some against you. The game is to encourage the development of behaviours and attitudes, in terms of mindset and beliefs, which work for you and to tackle and overcome those that work against you. It is all about being aware of what currently limits you and forms potential obstacles to your desired success.

Now I'm not saying that limiting beliefs can be overcome overnight as many of them have been with us since we were very young children, as my story earlier highlights. But it is like a person's weight: it generally creeps up slowly on them over a number of years until it reaches a point where they think 'I don't like the way I look and feel about my weight' so they decide to do something about it, starting to diet and exercise. The weight doesn't come off overnight, though. It took years for the weight to be put on so you can't expect it to disappear miraculously overnight. It is exactly the same with limiting behaviour and mindsets: they won't be changed overnight but they can be changed or better managed in time.

It's all about having a greater awareness of you. That means being aware of your tendencies to react in a certain way when it comes to money. Faced with this awareness, it then becomes a choice for you at that point. You are in a position to be making an informed response on how to balance your behaviour and likely reaction accordingly. Remember, evolution not revolution. Rome wasn't built in a day.

CHAPTER 5

What is profit?

Profit is the aim of the game for most businesses, otherwise what is the point of having to deal with all the curve balls that are frequently thrown at us as business owners? If you are in business purely for the love of what you do, then you can do what you do for enjoyment, perhaps as a hobby. You don't necessarily need the additional burden of dealing with everything that comes with running a business if that is your desired outcome.

The purpose of a business is to make money. It is how that profit is used that differentiates a private business from a charitable organisation. Both need to make a profit, though. The profits in a private company are generally utilised by the owner for whatever they choose, whereas the profits of a charity are used to re-invest and fund new services. Don't be mistaken; they must both make money to survive.

There are generally two types of profit that you will see frequently mentioned. They are *gross profit* and *net profit*. It is important that you understand the difference between the two of them.

Gross Profit

Gross profit is the difference between the selling price of a product or service and the *direct* costs taken to produce that product or service. These direct costs are also known as *variable costs.*

Variable costs are those costs that tend to fluctuate with the level of sales. They include, but are not limited to, such things as direct labour, raw materials, sales commissions and delivery expenses. They represent the *costs of the goods sold.*

At a whole business level, it is the difference between the sum of all the revenue generated from all sources and the sum of all the variable costs or direct costs of the goods sold to generate that revenue. It doesn't take into account the overheads or fixed costs of the business at this level; that happens in the next stage.

For example:

Revenue

Product 1 Type	*$50,000 (A)*
Product 2 Type	*$100,000 (B)*
Product 3 Type	*$200,000 (C)*
Total Revenue	$350,000 D (A + B + C)
Direct labour	*$50,000 (E)*
Raw materials	*$100,000 (F)*
Sales commissions	*$35,000 (G)*
Delivery expenses	*$15,000 (H)*
Total costs of good sold	$200,000 I (E + F + G + H)
Gross profit =	$150,000 J (D - I)

The *gross profit margin* expresses the gross profit amount as a percentage of revenue. In this case it is 42.9% (J /D x 100)

Net Profit

Net profit is the next layer down. It is the residual profit after all of the fixed costs or overheads of a business have been deducted.

Fixed costs are those costs that do not tend to fluctuate with the level of sales. They include, but are not limited to, such things as rent, equipment leases, insurance, interest on borrowed funds, business taxes and administrative salaries.

Gross profit from above = $150,000 (J)

Rent	*$20,000 (K)*
Equipment Leases	*$10,000 (L)*
Insurance	*$5,000 (M)*
Interest	*$5,000 (N)*
Administrative Salaries	*$40,000 (O)*

Total fixed costs/overheads $80,000 P (K + L + M + N + O)

Net profit = $70,000 Q (J - P)

The *net profit margin* expresses the net profit amount as a percentage of revenue. In this case it is 20.0% (Q/D x 100)

Look at it like a chocolate box containing 24 delicious-looking delights that represent your revenue. From that, you will need to offer some to others in exchange for the direct costs (variable) of producing that product or service. Say you need to give away sixteen of those chocolates to cover your variable costs. That leaves you with eight chocolates to cover your overheads.

Now, if you need more than eight chocolates to cover your fixed costs and overheads then you have nothing left to eat yourself. If you need less than eight chocolates to cover your overheads, then you get to eat the difference. Net profit is the chocolate that you get to keep and delight in yourself.

Gross profit represents the speed and ability of your business to cover its fixed costs and overheads and have something left over after all costs have been deducted. It follows that the higher your gross profit amount and margin, the quicker your business can cover its overheads and move into a net profit position. That's the desired outcome.

Revenue versus profitable revenue

There is a very important distinction between revenue and profitable revenue. Revenue is basically derived from whatever you charge your clients or customers for your products and services. You can charge anything you want but market forces usually cap it. By market forces I mean supply and demand in the segment of the market your business operates within.

Just because you have decided to charge a certain amount for your products and services is not a guarantee that you are making a profit on that revenue. Many business owners make the mistake of confusing revenue and profitable revenue and it is usually because of the ostrich mentality they have adopted, or the fact that they are scared of anything numbers related, that they haven't taken the time to actually sit down and work out whether they are making a profit on what they are charging or not.

Many of these same business owners are adopting the philosophy that as long as money is flowing into their bank account, all is well. The reality is that just because money is flowing into your bank account from revenue doesn't necessarily mean you are making a profit on it.

I remember as a young boy of twelve I became interested in vegetable gardening in a big way as I grew up in a rural area near Adelaide in Australia, surrounded by dairy farms and market gardens. I started with a small plot of about two metres by one metre but soon ran out of space. I wanted to grow more and a bigger area to grow them in, so I had an idea to grow seedlings and sell them to my Mum's nurse friends. I also knew some of them were into vegetable gardening so it was an opportunity for generating some cash to buy more stuff I needed for my garden. I charged $1.50 per punnet when the nurseries (garden centres) usually sold them for $2.50. I sold 37 of them in that lot for a sum total of $55.50. I was completely chuffed to bits.

But did I actually make any profit on that? I needed containers, soil, seeds, water and fertiliser to produce those punnets of vegetable seedlings. I largely used materials I already had to do this, but I did have to buy more supplies.

My point is that I was so focused on the amount of revenue I generated that to this day I don't know whether I actually made money or lost money in my little enterprise. I didn't sit down and work out what the costs would be to produce each punnet and whether what I was charging Mum's nursing colleagues was more than it cost me to grow the seedlings, leaving enough of a difference, i.e. the profit. I have never forgotten this lesson and thankfully I learned it very early on so was able to take this into my next enterprise at sixteen, which saw me generate enough profit to buy my first car – but more on that later.

There are two approaches that can be used to work out if your revenue is profitable to you or not. They are called the top-down approach and the bottom-up approach. I have tried to break it down in a simple way to illustrate and explain the process of completing the exercise. It is like anything: it can be made as complex or kept as simple as one chooses to make it. I don't know about you but I like to try and keep everything as simple as possible.

Top-down approach

As the name suggests, it entails starting at the top with the selling price and working down from there. It is more commonly used than the bottom-up approach. The three steps to do this are:

1. Ascertain market price – i.e. what price the market will accept.
2. Allocate desired profit margin.
3. Determine if the product or service can be provided within the net amount.

For the purposes of this exercise let's assume that you are looking to introduce a new product with the following information:

Scenario 1 – Top Down

- (P) = $50 per unit
- Desired Profit Margin = 40%
- Variable Cost (VC) - $35 per unit

STEP 1: The market price is $50

STEP 2: The desired profit margin is 40%, which means $20 per unit profit is desired ($50 x 40%)

STEP 3: The implied maximum cost allowance = $30 ($50 - $20)

Upon further investigation, the cost to produce this new product was shown to be possible at a variable cost of $35 per unit. As $35 is greater than the implied maximum cost of $30, you are faced with one of three options:

1. Review all the information again to ensure that no further favourable changes can be made to either the market price or cost to produce.
2. Reduce profit margin expectations, which means that more products will need to be sold to achieve break-even when overheads are factored in.
3. Or you can pass on the new product idea completely because the numbers don't stack up to meet your expectations.

The important thing here is that by doing this exercise a rational and informed decision can be made on how best to take the business forward in a profitable way. It is not reliant on chance or luck.

Bottom-up approach

The bottom-up approach is the reverse of the top-down approach. The three steps to do this are:

1. Determine the cost.
2. Add the desired profit margin or mark up.
3. This determines the selling price.

Scenario 2 – Bottom Up

- Variable cost = $40 per unit
- Desired mark up = 25%

STEP 1: The cost in this case has been determined at $40 per unit

STEP 2: Work out the desired mark up amount, which is $10 in this case ($40 x 25%)

STEP 3: Add the results from Step 1 and 2 together for an indicative selling price for that product of $50 ($40 + $10)

You can then test whether this $50 selling price is acceptable to the market in which you operate. If it is, then great, you could be on to something that meets your profit expectations and the market wants. Everybody is happy.

I shared with you earlier my seedling story. To continue from where I left off, I was so determined not to make the same mistake in my next endeavour that I learned from my first experience. This time it was something bigger to play for – my first car. I wanted to do it myself and I wanted to make $1,000 to buy it.

I remember going to the native plant nursery (garden centre) with my Mum and noticing the price of plants. There was one type in particular that grabbed my attention. That plant was called a Sturt Desert Pea. If you don't know what it is, don't worry, not many people do outside of Australia. A Sturt Desert Pea is the state emblem of South Australia. It has a really striking red and black flower.

Anyway they were selling them for $12.50 and I figured that with my green thumb I could do it myself and sell them for a lower price of $10.00. I did some more research and asked lots of questions and felt confident that it was worth giving it a go. This time, though, I sat down and worked out what else I would need other than what I had and precisely what it would cost. I worked out it would cost me approximately $2.00 per plant for the extra materials I would need. The numbers I worked to were as follows:

Target amount needed for my car:	$1,000

Target selling price:	$10.00
Cost to produce:	$2.00
Profit per plant:	$8.00

This meant that I would have to produce and sell 125 plants ($1,000 / $8 profit per pot).

So to cut a long story short, I used some of my savings to buy the materials I needed. There ended up being plants everywhere, but I did what I set out to do. I sold the plants to family, friends and Mum's work colleagues again. At the end of it, I had the $1,000 I needed to buy my first car. It wasn't the best car in the world and was bright orange, but it was all mine and I had paid for every part of it. I was a proud young man. I wasn't leaving making the money I sought to chance and neither should you by ignoring your numbers.

Setting profit targets

Setting profit targets are important markers for progress against your business plan. They provide you with the financial road map you need to achieve on a monthly or quarterly basis. They break the bigger financial goals of your business into smaller, more short-term goals which, if met, means that the annual target will be met.

It's just like when you set out on an extended road trip in your car. You start with an intended destination in mind. You know where you are heading but it is likely that you will have certain points that you know you need to get to, so that you remain on schedule to get to the place you are going at precisely the time you intended to arrive there.

When setting targets it is important that they are SMART targets. The same principle applies to setting effective goals. SMART stands for the following:

S – SPECIFIC — You need to express the profit target as an identifiable amount. You need to know exactly what you are aiming for.

M – MEASURABLE — You need to be able to track the result. This will generally come from the Profit and Loss statement, which should be produced regularly on either a monthly or quarterly basis, together with other key information with which to manage the business.

A – ACHIEVABLE — It needs to be 'doable' given the state of the business and the resources available to pursue it.

R – REALISTIC — Similar to achievable, it needs to be possible in light of potential obstacles and constraints known at the time of setting the target.

T – TIMED — It needs to have a time period attached to it. Annual profit targets should be set as an absolute minimum.

The preference is for shorter time horizons as they are generally less daunting then big scary targets. Without a time period attached it remains open-ended, so there is no deadline by which the target needs to be met so therefore no real impetus to 'go for it'.

It is vitally important that you continuously check your progress against the targets you have set, otherwise how will you know if you are on track or not? If you are falling behind, then by tracking and monitoring your progress you are able to identify any reasons for falling behind schedule and take corrective action that will see you back on track.

Consider the stop points you planned for your road trip. You watched the speedometer and were able to assess your progress each time you arrived at each stop. Were you ahead of schedule or behind schedule? Did you need to pick up pace or did you have plenty of time between this and the next stop? Did you need to alter your course because of a road diversion that you didn't anticipate?

By tracking and monitoring performance against profit targets you are in the driving seat. You are in the position of control, which means you can make choices based on what circumstance presents itself at each checkpoint. It's about you controlling the process and not letting the process control you. Doing this means that you are not leaving reaching the targets to chance; you are being proactive in ensuring that they stand the best chance of being met.

Profit under the spotlight

In business the emphasis is on getting more CUSTOMERS, growing REVENUE and generating PROFIT. But there is a subtle distinction that needs to be made here. These areas are actually 'results'. They are the end product of certain activities. Strictly speaking they can't be altered directly. You can't simply get more customers, revenue or profit.

There are in fact other factors that determine these results, so to change these results we need to understand and focus on the underlying factors that influence these results. Let's look at the steps involved in closer detail.

STEP 1:   You identify through marketing or other means people that are **potentially** interested in your products and services.

STEP 2:   You have sales conversations with them and they decide whether to buy your products and services or not. If they do proceed, it is at this point that they become a CUSTOMER.

STEP 3:   Once they have decided to buy from you a transaction will take place at the time they buy, whatever they are seeking.

STEP 4:   They will pay a certain price for that transaction to occur and receive the products and services they are seeking. It is the transaction and price paid for that transaction that results in the REVENUE generated from that customer.

STEP 5:   Provided you have priced your revenue properly, you will generate a margin on that revenue. It is the margin on revenue you generated that ultimately determines the PROFIT you make from that particular customer.

So it follows that if the desired result is to increase overall PROFIT then you need to be talking to more people who are potentially in the market for the products or services you provide and you need to get more of them to say 'yes'. Of those that say 'yes' and become a customer, you need to encourage them to buy more frequently from you, spend more with you each time they do buy from you and ensure that you are making a decent margin on the revenue you are generating. That's how you grow profits. I hope you can see the underlying logic of this.

If we take it a step further, from the five steps we covered, there are five key areas to focus on to grow profits, which can be summarised as follows:

KEY FOCUS 1:   Number of leads
KEY FOCUS 2:   Conversion rate
KEY FOCUS 3:   Number of transactions
KEY FOCUS 4:   Average sale value
KEY FOCUS 5:   Margin

Profit Accelerator Formula

Each of the five key focus areas interacts in what I call the Profit Accelerator Formula as follows:

Number of leads (1)

x

Conversion rate (2)

=

NUMBER OF CUSTOMERS

x

Number of transactions (3)

x

Average sale value (4)

=

REVENUE

x

Margin (5)

=

PROFIT

Don't worry, it's okay if you are a bit confused at this point. We will cover each of these five focus areas in more detail over the coming chapters. I promise you that it will make more sense to you when we bring it all together with a case study in Chapter 11 which shows just how powerful this information is for transforming your understanding and therefore the profits of your business.

I hope you are starting to feel just a little bit excited. If you're not, then you definitely should be as what we are about to cover will change the way you look at profit forever...

CHAPTER 6

Key Focus 1 –
Number of Leads

Number of Leads (1)

x

Conversion Rate (2)

=

NUMBER OF CUSTOMERS

This is the total number of potential buyers that you contacted or who contacted you in the last year, also known as prospects or potentials.

Most business owners confuse responses, or the number of potential buyers, with results. Just because the phone is ringing doesn't mean the cash register is.

And what is even more amazing is that very few businesses even know how many leads they get a week, let alone from each and every marketing campaign.

A lead generation strategy is basically your marketing strategy. The purpose of a marketing strategy is to reach new pools of potential clients that may be willing buyers of your products and services.

Before we get into some ideas for things you can do to improve your number of leads there are seven things to keep in mind when putting a lead generation strategy into action.

Be targeted in your marketing activities

A scattergun approach rarely works and can be a complete waste of your marketing money. You should be very clear on the profile and demographics of your ideal client. You need to determine their habits and behaviours, which includes understanding the things they like to do, read and watch. The goal here is to focus your marketing activities on those areas that your ideal client will be exposed to as they go about their daily lives.

Set your objectives before undertaking the strategy

This involves understanding the reasons why a particular marketing activity is being undertaken. If you don't set objectives then how can you know whether the strategy has been successful or not?

Be clear on the outcome you're seeking

You must have a desired outcome in mind. It involves being clear on what you are expecting your target audience to do as a result of the communication. Is the desired outcome that they sign up for a mailing list? Purchase a particular product? Register for a newsletter? Be clear on the action and response you expect.

Test and measure

This is a big one and an area in which most businesses fail miserably. It is important to determine whether a particular strategy will deliver the intended results or not before embarking on a massive campaign. This involves starting with smaller test campaigns to see how effective it will be.

Often subtle changes to the wording or colours used can have a dramatic impact on the results. Try them on a small scale to begin with and measure the results. For example, say you are looking at producing a flyer. You may have six versions of an advert with different wording and look and feel. It is best to do restricted tests within a distribution area which represents a subset of the overall market you are targeting. The responses to each small test campaign with different wording and content will vary and from that you can identify what works best, refine it further and keep testing until you crack the winning formula that delivers a more positive result.

You should do this testing, measuring and refining cycle before committing to a huge campaign. When you think about it, what is the point of getting carried away with committing to the time and expense of jumping in the deep end with, say, a 100,000 run of flyers when the likely outcome is completely unknown? By doing smaller runs of, say, 500 flyers and measuring the results as you go, you are not throwing away unnecessary money. Marketing is a science as well as an art. It needs to be approached in a methodical and deliberate manner.

The key message to remember here is that the only way you can know whether a marketing campaign is working or not is to test the options and then measure and track the results. How will you know otherwise? It's just like when we try a new food. We usually have a taste first and if we like it, then we feel confident to have more of it. The same principle applies here.

Ensure you are getting a decent return on your marketing investment

Many business owners make the mistake of viewing marketing as a cost. It is a common reaction in leaner times that marketing is one of the first areas that a business will cut back on. For me, this represents flawed thinking and is a silly decision to be making. Targeted and effective marketing represents the future sales pipeline of your business. Why then would you choose to cut back on the very area that will generate future revenue?

In my opinion, marketing must be viewed as an investment and as with any investments, there can be good and bad ones. Take a share portfolio for instance. Contained within that are a number of different types of shares and some of those will be performing better than others in the portfolio.

It is only by tracking and measuring the performance of those shares that you can determine which are performing better and which aren't. Part of portfolio management involves letting the good investments run and getting rid of the bad. When investing, we are told that a balanced portfolio is the desired objective. This means holding a number of different shares in the portfolio to diversify our risk so that if one investment performs badly, then the good performance of other shares helps offset the bad performance. It's all about not having all of our eggs in the same basket. If we drop that basket and all the eggs break, then we have nothing left.

The exact same investing principles apply to marketing. We need to have a balanced portfolio of marketing activities within our business so that we are not reliant on just one. We need to know what is working and what isn't by constantly monitoring the results by testing and measuring.

We want to stop the marketing activities that aren't working and do more of the marketing activities that are working. People and markets evolve. Something that is working one month may not necessarily work as effectively in another month. Having a portfolio of things that we do helps balance out this impact.

The distinction here is between conscious marketing and unconscious marketing. Conscious marketing is deliberate targeted marketing and should be seen as an investment. Like any investment, we expect to receive a return on our investment that is acceptable to us. Unconscious marketing that is not deliberate, not targeted and not measured is actually a cost and should be stopped immediately.

If a strategy isn't delivering the intended results after giving it a good go – cut your losses and move on. Time is money

Don't be scared to stop doing something that isn't working. As with investing, if a share price is performing poorly and you are losing money on it, there reaches a point where you need to cut your losses and redirect your resources into finding an alternative. Frequently, business owners fall into the trap of doing what they have always done. They continue to do something because they have become used to doing it.

Don't get emotionally attached to a particular marketing activity. It must be viewed as an investment decision. If something is not delivering the intended results then stop doing it immediately, cut your losses and move on to identifying the next initiative to try.

If something isn't generating the desired result, then it is lunacy is to keep doing it because it is what you have always done and to expect a different result.

Be creative and have fun with it!

You should see marketing as a game. It is a game that you can have fun with, thinking up new ideas that are innovative and creative for reaching your ideal clients. Be bold and go for it. The real value to a business lies in the execution of the ideas. Remember, conscious marketing!

PRE-EXERCISE HEADS UP

I want you to think about your business as you read through the 25 ideas for increasing the number of leads in your business that we are about to cover. Your task at the end of it will be to brainstorm five ideas for ways that you can improve the number of leads you are generating by 25% in the next year. So simply bear this in mind as you read through the possible ideas over the coming pages.

There will be space after this section for you to write down the five ideas you have come up with that you think could help you generate 25% more leads over the next year, so just have your thinking head fully engaged and on for now.

25 ideas to help get you started

An important thing to note is that some of the ideas may not be applicable or relevant for your business, but that's okay. The ideas provided are designed to stimulate your thinking and some ideas may apply to more than one focus area.

1.   Strategic alliances and joint ventures

This involves working together with other businesses that are not your competitors and have common objectives. This is where you help each other get more business for each of your businesses. It's all about creating mutual benefit and a win/win situation for all involved.

2.   Referrals

Give to get – it isn't one-sided. Don't just take all of the time. Make referrals to others freely and you will find that in time you will get more back this way, as you will be remembered and the receiving party will usually go above and beyond in their desire to return the favour.

3.   Host beneficiary

This is where you promote your products and services directly to the customers of another business. There are many different ways to do this, such as offering a gift voucher for your business that is from the owner of the other business, or offering the other business owner a commission on any sales.

4.   Yellow pages, white pages and other local directories

The old paper directories used to be the way we would seek whatever services we were looking for. Then along came the internet and it displaced some of the more traditional ways of having a business listed. There is definitely still a place for inclusion in directories, though, especially online directories. Many online directories are free and can drive traffic directly to your website.

Remember, it is about completely understanding the profile and demographics of your target clients. It's about understanding what they do, where they visit and what they read, so you can identify the best medium to reach them.

Older people, for example, generally aren't always as confident and internet savvy as their younger counterparts, so if this is your market then the traditional paper directories are likely to be more appropriate than the online ones. There is no 'one size fits all' approach to this.

5.   Press releases

Spreading the word. Press releases, both online and traditional offline, generally cost very little to produce and distribute but can make a massive difference for the exposure of a business if done in the right way. When it works well, money can usually never buy the equivalent advertising that has the same impact and reach as a properly executed press release. Editors want relevant, informative and interesting content for their readers. Produce that for them and they will love you and your business will benefit from the exposure as a result.

6.   Social media

Social media is all about interaction and positioning yourself as an expert in what you do. Better-known platforms are Linked in, Facebook, Google Plus and Twitter. There are loads more, though. Having a social media strategy is becoming increasingly important for many businesses to keep up and communicate with a changing marketplace.

7.   DIY direct mail or email

This involves contacting people who may be potentially interested in your products and services directly by sending them something in the mail or by using email. The people you contact can either be known or unknown to you.

Buying the use of databases and mailing lists is a common way of accessing people that are unknown to you. Be warned, though, that response rates are typically low so don't expect too much. Also be very wary of the quality of the information you are buying. It is important to buy only from credible sources. Above all, do not SPAM! It is illegal to SPAM and could land you in very hot water.

8. **Networking functions**

We covered my experiences with this back in Chapter 1. There are many different options here which include things like speed networking, informal networking, structured networking and breakfast networking.

The key is identifying what works best for you, having a concise pitch and approaching networking with a view to **not getting sales directly from it**. The focus needs to be on expanding your network of contacts through nurturing and building enduring relationships with people over time that is based on trust and integrity. Remember, people do business with people.

Now, you may not end up doing business with that person but you don't know who they know who could be the ideal client you are looking for. Invest in building relationships with relevant people. Those relationships will be key to building a sustainable and enduring business. Generally, it's not what you know that matters but who you know and who knows you that counts. Keep an open mind always and don't pre-judge someone.

9. **Seminars and events**

Become a speaker on your topic – once again this could provide instant credibility if you know what you're talking about and, of course, deliver a solid presentation.

10. **Trade shows**

Again, make sure it is related to your target market. Perhaps get a stand yourself, it is good way to network with other stand-holders where there could be potential for strategic alliances and joint ventures that are mutually beneficial to all parties moving forward.

11. **Piggyback invoice mailings**

When sending out invoices include a special offer flyer. Any promotional material could be sent with your invoices or you could negotiate for your special offer flyer to be included in the invoice mailings of other businesses.

12. **In-store, footpath & building signage**

This is all about letting the world know that you are there. Make your business known visually to passing traffic. Utilise void or wasted space to your advantage.

13. **Distributors or agents**

Distributors or agents usually have a huge network of

connections to distribute products, in particular, for qualifying businesses to access. It is important that you find the right distributor or agent that is aligned with the goals and objectives of your business and be sure to read the fine print so there are no surprises down the line. You usually pay a fee or percentage commission to them under such an arrangement, but it is generally done on a success basis so that no fees are payable unless the results are produced.

14. Licensees or franchisees

Could you perhaps franchise your business and bring other people in to work under your brand in a controlled way to expand into new geographic markets?

15. Fridge magnets or car signage

It's about being seen so that you are in the forefront of the minds of your target audience. For example, say you ran a plumbing business and you provided a specific area that you cover with fridge magnets with your contact information on them. Now, if their pipes spring a leak and your magnet was on their fridge, who do you think they are more likely to call? The same principle applies for car signage and other trinkets that people use – it's about being seen and staying on top of the pile so that when the need arises, they immediately think of you and pick up the phone.

16. Window displays

It is been shown that attractive and inviting window displays draw customers into a retail business. Be bold, creative and alluring to potential customers so that your business stands out to passing traffic.

17. Television, radio or press advertising

Radio and press advertising is a cheaper alternative to television advertising which is usually beyond the means of most small businesses. Television advertising is more suited to brand awareness and mass-market consumer brands. Be targeted in your approach and know what your target audience is reading and watching.

18. Run a competition

Run and promote a competition with a desirable prize for your target audience. The competition may require a purchase in-store or some other action to be taken to enter. This could mean a potential new source of customers or clients for a business whilst raising its profile indirectly.

19. Internet/web pages

This a big subject area in its own right and includes such things as Search Engine Optimisation (SEO) for your website, Pay-Per-Click (PPC) advertising and much more. I believe that every business should have an online presence, however basic. It must portray the right image of the business, though, as a dodgy-looking website can do more harm than good.

20. Salespeople, cold calling and telemarketing

This involves either employing others to fulfil the selling function in your business or using outsourced third party service providers to act on your behalf and contact potential customers, generally in an unsolicited way.

As we have covered numerous times already, and I'm going to keep emphasising the message, the more targeted you are in understanding the buying habits and profile of your target client, the more tailored your approach can be. This should increase the likelihood of a more successful outcome.

21. Write a book

Get published. Be seen as the expert in your field. This usually provides instant credibility and results in people coming to you because of it. Pre-sell them in your book to the idea of doing business with you.

22. Tender lists

There are numerous websites and publications to which a business can subscribe to receive details of opportunities for work that both government and private enterprises are seeking. For the right type of business, these lists could be an ideal platform for identifying new opportunities to quote for.

23. Trade longer or different hours

Give your clients or potential clients what they want. It is about understanding and catering to their lifestyle and buying habits. This would also differentiate you from your competitors and give you a point of difference in the eyes of your clients and potential clients.

24. Business cards

Often a business card is overlooked as a marketing tool. However, it is hugely powerful as it is commonly the first item that is exchanged when meeting someone new. Make sure it is clear when someone looks at your business card that they get a sense of what business you are in. Remember, business cards have a front and a back.

25. Catalogues

Produce a catalogue of your products, or get into someone else's catalogue to show what you offer to your target audience. It is about educating customers about what you sell and how you can meet their needs.

JUST FOR FUN EXERCISE

STEP 1

I hope these ideas help stimulate some thoughts on what you could do in your business. So, now I want you to think about your business specifically. Your task is to brainstorm five ideas for ways that you can improve the number of leads you are generating by 25% in the next year.

You should be asking yourself, "How could I be reaching 25% more potential clients than I am currently?" That means if the number of leads you generate each year is 1,000, the exercise is to come up with ideas that can see this rise by 250 to 1,250 in the next year.

Now, if you can't think of five ideas then you aren't thinking hard enough and need to try harder! I want you to be bold in your thinking. Be creative and have fun with it.

IDEA 1
_____

_____

_____

IDEA 2
_____

_____

_____

IDEA 3
_____

_____

_____

IDEA 4
_____

_____

_____

IDEA 5
_____

_____

_____

STEP 2

Now I want you to give the five top ideas that you have brainstormed a mark out of 10 that reflects the likely effectiveness, the confidence you have to do it, the availability of resources to implement it and the likely results.

IDEA 1 _____ / 10

IDEA 2 _____ / 10

IDEA 3 _____ / 10

IDEA 4 _____ / 10

IDEA 5 _____ / 10

It's important that you do not move on from this chapter until you complete the ideas and rank them as instructed. All will make sense later in the book.

So, in this chapter we have covered the first of the five key focus areas.

It's great to get a lot of leads, but then you've got to remember your conversion rate.

CHAPTER 7

Key Focus 2 –
Conversion Rate

Number of Leads (1)

x

Conversion Rate (2)

=

NUMBER OF CUSTOMERS

Your conversion rate is the percentage of people who did actually buy from you as opposed to those who could have bought. For example, if you had ten people walk through your store today and you sold to only three of them, you'd have a conversion rate of three out of ten, or 30%.

Imagine you're on a basketball court and you have a limit of ten attempts to get the ball through the hoop. If only four of those balls go through the hoop then the conversion rate between the actual number of times it went through the hoop and the total number of tries you had is 40% (four successful attempts out of a total of ten possible attempts).

In business, the conversion rate is worked out by dividing the number of people who say 'yes' to buying what you offer against the total number of people you have communicated with about potentially buying from you. Do you see the distinction? If you don't, then slowly read the last couple of paragraphs again and hopefully it will make more sense.

This is a literal gold mine of opportunity for any business. A business simply needs to get more of their leads or potential customers to say 'yes' and become actual customers by buying something from them!

You may not realise this yet, but by doubling your conversion rate, you double the number of customers that are buying from you! Let me show you how this works. Say you have

1,000 leads and a conversion rate of 25% and you manage to double that conversion rate to 50%, your actual number of buying customers increases from 250 to 500. That's double!

Frequently many businesses over estimate their conversion rate as they fail to measure it. The actual reality is usually much lower when measured.

Do you measure your conversion rate? Do you know what it is with a high degree of accuracy?

PRE-EXERCISE HEADS UP

I want you to think about your business as you read through the 25 ideas for improving the conversion rate in your business that we are about to cover. Your task at the end of it will be to brainstorm five ideas for ways that you can improve the conversion rate you are achieving by 25% in the next year. So simply bear this in mind as you read through the possible ideas over the coming pages.

There will be space after this section for you to write down the five ideas you have come up with that could help you improve your conversion rate by 25% over the next year, so just have your thinking head fully engaged and on for now.

An important thing to note is that some of the ideas may not be applicable or relevant for your business, but that's okay. The ideas provided are designed to stimulate your thinking and some ideas may apply to more than one focus area.

25 ideas to help get you started

1. Set sales targets

Give your sales team a clear idea of what you need them to achieve. Sales scripts and training are also important. The trick with scripts is to identify by testing and measuring what works and what doesn't. The elements that work should be used again and the elements that don't work discarded. This process of refining continues until an effective working script is achieved. A well-executed script delivers results consistently time and time again. It is a case of working out what works and repeating it.

2. Measure conversion rates

How do you know what your conversion rate is if you don't measure it? The very act of measuring something puts it in focus and allows a platform for future improvements.

3. Define your uniqueness

Create a point of difference in the eyes of potential customers or clients. Communicate that point of difference widely, which could involve including the vision you have for your business in material that goes out to clients. Let the world know what your business stands for and why they should do business with you.

4. Build trust and rapport

Remember, people do business with people. Good relationships are key. We are more likely to buy from someone we know and trust or if somebody we know and trust recommends something to us.

5. Print a benefits and testimonials list

Educate your customers on why they should buy from you and back it up with quotes from satisfied customers. People generally like third party validation. It helps reassure them that they are doing the right thing, which is especially important if you are unknown to them.

6. Take credit cards, debit cards and cheques

The aim here is to make it easy for people to give you their money through offering a variety of payment methods. This extends to possibly using payment plans and offering financing if appropriate.

7. Demonstrations

Show people how your products could be used. Make it easy and familiar for them. This could take the form of in-store, audio or even video sales demonstrations. People generally like to try things before they buy. It provides reassurance to them.

8. Use prospect questionnaires

Find out what your customers want and make it available to them. It's a logical assumption to make that if you provide your target audience with the products and services they need and that solves a problem for them, they are more likely to buy that solution which means a higher expected conversion rate.

9.   **Up-sell, cross-sell and down-sell**

Up-selling is a sales technique where a salesperson encourages the customer to purchase more expensive items, upgrades or other add-ons in an attempt to make a more profitable sale. Cross-selling involves the sale of an additional product or service to an existing customer from your range. Down-selling is often used to prevent a non-sale situation by suggesting a less expensive or alternative product to secure a sale.

Be creative in coming up with solutions for your clients. Think of other products and services you offer that may be suitable given the identified need. Understanding the underlying need and meeting that need lessens any resistance to the client saying 'yes, I'll take it'.

10.   **Follow up and follow up again**

Have a communication strategy around dealing with new enquiries and leads. Make people feel special and loved. Be diligent in following up but don't be annoying! Also, always do what you say you are going to do. If you promise somebody something by a particular time and date, then make sure you stick to that promise. It builds trust, rapport and confidence in the prospect so they know that you won't let them down.

11.   **Ask for the sale**

It might sound obvious but many businesses simply fail to ask for the sale. Be bold. You won't know the answer unless you ask the question.

12. **Written Guarantee**

It helps take some risk out of the buying decision if buyers know that they have some recourse if they are not happy or what you offer doesn't live up to expectations. Here's a little secret: most guarantees are never called in so don't be too worried about making big bold guarantees.

13. **A gift voucher towards purchase and other special offers**

Offer a special offer to encourage buying. Make sure there is a time limit attached to it to create a sense of urgency. Common applications are discounts on first purchase, or a special one-time offer on a particular product or service that your research shows they would potentially be interested in.

14. **Scarcity and limits**

Introduce some element of scarcity and limits around a promotion. No one likes to feel they are going to miss out on something.

15. **Rewrite your quotes, tenders and proposals into action plans**

Be different and make it easy for your clients to see and understand the value that your business brings to achieving their desired outcomes. By presenting these as action plans, the buying resistance is reduced as you are providing them with the exact recipe and ingredients to solve their 'problem'.

16. Sell on emotion and dreams

Connect with the emotional needs of the client and the reasons for a purchase. Customers generally need an emotional connection to buy.

17. Provide team incentives

Incentivise your team to perform and improve conversion rates by rewarding them for doing so. Employees generally respond more positively to doing something if they can see a direct benefit to them for doing so. Make sure that any incentives are aligned to a profitable outcome for your business, though. That's the critical bit!

18. Survey

Put together a survey that specifically targets your potential clients. People love being asked to give their opinion! Give them an incentive or 'thank you' for completing the survey such as a gift voucher towards purchase. Create the survey questions carefully so that you gain valuable insights which can be used to build a relationship with them for a potential future purchase.

19. Try before you buy

People like to touch, feel and smell things so give potential customers the opportunity to do just that. It helps remove the risk that a product or service might not be right for the customer and lowers the resistance for a sale to happen. For example, if you sell vacuum cleaners then let them try one themselves to see how good it is. Let them experience how much better their life will be as a result of purchasing that particular product.

20. Target better prospects

If you understand the complete profile of your target ideal client, including what they like, their buying habits and the problem for which you have a solution, then if you centre your marketing activities around reaching that profile of customer, they will be more inclined to purchase from you because your product or service meets their identified need.

So instead of being a cold prospect when they are contacted, they are more likely to be a warm prospect and therefore more inclined to be interested in what you are offering. Better quality prospects will translate into better results.

21. Increase product knowledge

You and your selling team must know everything about your entire product range. If this isn't the case then further training on this area is vital. You are being looked to as the expert and if you can't answer specific questions or appear vague then it will completely undermine your credibility in the eyes of the person seeking your help. This means that they will be less likely to purchase from your business. You absolutely must be able to answer customer queries fully and with confidence.

22. Packaging

Superficially, we all generally judge something, at least initially, on the way it looks. Be honest; think about the people you meet. We make a snap instant decision about that person based on the way they look, whether we do it consciously or not. It is the same for packaging: if something looks horrible, then what reason is there to buy it? But if something is pleasant on the eye then we are more likely to be interested enough to find out more information. Generally, the more attractive the product looks, the better chance there is of selling it.

23.   On-hold phone messages

You should utilise every opportunity you have with a potential or existing customer to reassure them that they made the right decision in trusting you with their purchase. Such an opportunity exists when they phone your business. Impressions count. Use the time when your customers are on hold to you to tell them about your products and services and reasons why they should buy from you, instead of leaving them to endure tacky music.

24.   Sell your own product line or an exclusive line

This is a really good one if it is possible within the scope of your business. It results in an almost 100% conversion rate. It's where you create something or stock a range of products that is sold exclusively by your business. That means it is not available anywhere else, so if your clients or potential new clients want that product or service, they have no option than to come to you for it.

If your business is a service type business, then you need to offer exclusivity in some way and a real point of difference which isn't available anywhere else. Be creative and solve the problems and needs of your target clients in a way that they can't get anywhere else.

25. Store or office appearance

First impressions do count and a̤ matter. People are judging, whether consᴄᵢₑ unconsciously, every aspect of their interaction with you in deciding whether to trust you to solve their problem. So have high dress standards and a clean, uncluttered and organised store or office.

The aim is to make people feel comfortable, welcome and build confidence that you are the right person to help them meet their needs. It's about always projecting the right image that fits your products or services.

JUST FOR FUN EXERCISE

STEP 1

I hope the ideas helped stimulate some thoughts on what you could do in your business. So, I want you to think about your business specifically. Your task is to brainstorm five ideas for ways that you can improve the conversion rate in your business by 25% in the next year.

You should be asking yourself, "How could I have 25% more of my potential clients say 'yes' and buy something from me in the next year?" That means if currently 100 in every 1,000 (10%) are saying 'yes' to you, then what can you do to increase this by 25 to 125 in every 1,000 (12.5%) in the next year?

Now, if you can't think of five ideas then you aren't thinking hard enough and need to try harder! I want you to be bold in your thinking. Be creative and have fun with it.

IDEA 1

_____

_____

_____

IDEA 2

_____

_____

_____

IDEA 3

_____

_____

_____

IDEA 4

_____

_____

_____

IDEA 5

_____

_____

_____

STEP 2

Now I want you to give the five top ideas that you have brainstormed a mark out of 10 that reflects the likely effectiveness, the confidence you have to do it, the availability of resources to implement it and the likely results.

IDEA 1 _____ / 10

IDEA 2 _____ / 10

IDEA 3 _____ / 10

IDEA 4 _____ / 10

IDEA 5 _____ / 10

It's important that you do not move on from this chapter until you complete the ideas and rank them as instructed. All will make sense later in the book.

So, in this chapter we have covered the second of the five key focus areas. It is the combining of the two factors we covered in this chapter and the preceding chapter that determines the number of customers who have purchased from your business over a set period of time.

Remember that the number of customers is a RESULT, which can't be influenced directly. This result can only be changed by focusing on what influences the result, which in this case is the number of leads being generated and the conversion rate being achieved.

Number of Leads (1)

x

Conversion Rate (2)

=

NUMBER OF CUSTOMERS

The result represents the number of different customers you deal with. You work it out by multiplying the total number of leads by the conversion rate.

Remember, it's not about getting *more customers or clients.* You can't change that number directly. It's about getting more leads and then improving your conversion rate. These are the areas to focus on to improve the result.

CHAPTER 8

Key Focus 3 – Number of transactions

NUMBER OF CUSTOMERS
x
Number of transactions (3)
x
Average sale value (4)
=
REVENUE

Some of your customers or clients will buy from you weekly, others monthly, others on the odd occasion and others just once in a lifetime. What you want to know now is the average – not your best and not your worst but the average number of times one of your customers buys from you in a year.

Take the act of grocery shopping. We all usually do it daily, weekly or monthly. Each time we go to do our grocery shop this is considered a 'transaction' and it is usually triggered by us running out of certain foods. We need to replenish our fridges and cupboards with the food and things that satisfy our needs for the next period until we run out again. But we generally have a choice of which of the big supermarket chains we go to shop at. If we aren't happy with something or have a bad experience, then we go elsewhere. The same principle applies with your business.

The number of transactions represents the frequency with which a customer purchases from you in a given period. If their experience with you is bad, then they will look elsewhere and are therefore less inclined to buy from you again. Oh, and be warned, they will usually share that they have had a bad experience with many other people, which could be fatal for your business, especially now we are in the age of social media.

People are generally less inclined to share details of a positive experience and definitely more likely to share details of a bad experience. It's human nature. Where's the drama and story in a good experience? Bad experiences tick all the boxes in that respect. The old rule of thumb was that if someone had a good buying experience they might tell one other person, but if they had a bad experience then they would tell ten. Now think about Facebook and Twitter alone, where most people usually have hundreds or thousands of friends or followers. In this case, all that person needs to do is post a message about their bad experience and those hundreds and thousands of friends or followers will know instantly. What happens if those contacts then share that with their networks?

My point here is that we are in a new age of interacting online and one bad experience could quite easily be spread by posting a simple message online which can be seen by hundreds, thousands or even millions of people. Think about the impact something like that could have on your business if one bad experience is being shared like this. It is really quite sobering when you think about it, which is why you must be on top of your game.

The aim of the game here is to encourage your customers or clients to keep coming back and spending their money with you regularly by providing them with a compelling reason to do so.

PRE-EXERCISE HEADS UP

I want you to think about your business as you read through the 25 ideas for improving the number of transactions in your business that we are about to cover. Your task at the end of it will be to brainstorm five ideas for ways that you can improve the number of transactions you are achieving by 25% over the next year. So simply bear this in mind as you read through the possible ideas over the coming pages.

There will be space after this section for you to write down the five ideas you have come up with that you think could help you improve your number of transactions by 25% over the next year, so just have your thinking hat on.

An important thing to note is that some of the ideas may not be applicable or relevant for your business, but that's okay. The ideas provided are designed to stimulate your thinking and some ideas may apply to more than one focus area.

25 ideas to help get you started

1.   Under promise and over deliver

Surprise your customers by consistently exceeding their expectations. They will not only keep coming back for more, time and time again, but they will become raving advocates for your business.

2.   Keep clients' vital information

The aim here is to keep an up-to-date database of information so that you really get to know your clients and can provide a more tailored service to meet their exact needs consistently. Having this good information enables you to target likely repeat purchasers. This involves keeping relevant and targeted information on present and past customers.

3. Timetable of communication

Just like you would stay in touch with your friends, you need to stay in touch with your clients. Find out what they are doing and share with them what you are doing. Have a structured strategy for regularly and consistently communicating with your customers, which may involve sending out a regular newsletter, tips or phoning them every now and then.

Keep your customers updated on the areas they have expressed an interest in by purchasing your products and services in the past and remind them why they need to come back and buy from you again by providing them with a compelling reason to do so. It overcomes the 'out of sight, out of mind' phenomenon.

4. Deliver consistently and reliably

This is about doing what you say you will and doing it to the satisfaction of your clients every single time. You must always meet their expectations, it is the only way to build trust and create loyalty. Take the global fast food chain McDonalds for instance; you can be assured that whenever you buy one of their burgers, it will always taste and look the same every single time. You can have confidence going into any McDonalds and knowing what you will get.

What about when you need a haircut? You tend to go to the same barber or hairdresser every single time because they know how you like your hair cut or styled. You go back because you have confidence that you can rely on them to cut your hair just the way you like it on each occasion. If they ever do a bad haircut, you may forgive them the first time but if it continues to happen then you will look elsewhere and tell everybody about the bad experience you have had.

Most people don't like change so when they do find a product or service that works for them and always meets their expectations they are more likely to buy again than look elsewhere when the need arises. The key is to become to destination of choice for a customer when they need what you offer.

5. **Post-purchase reassurance**

People like to feel they are being taken care of, so in subtle ways keep telling your customers that they did the right thing in buying from you. Don't forget about them once the sale is complete; look after them and make sure they are happy with whatever they have purchased. They won't forget you if you do this.

6. **Closed-door sales**

Make your customers feel that they are part of an exclusive club by offering them special deals ahead of other people.

7. **Co-operative promotions**

This involves working in collaboration with other businesses to undertake promotions together for mutual benefit. This works well with businesses that have different offerings which complement each other. Remember, you are looking to find a win/win situation that gives your clients what they need and the businesses involved what they are seeking.

8. **Run a frequent buyers' programme or VIP card**

We've all seen them and probably have many different loyalty cards in our wallets. The purpose of these cards is to encourage repeat spending and reward customers for doing so by providing special incentives and special offers. Be creative and different with it. If done well, the programme itself can become your point of difference that distinguishes you from your competitors in the eyes of your ideal clients.

9. **Inform customers of your entire range**

Often customers come to a business with one reason in mind, which is centred on their current need. Often they can have tunnel vision with regard to that need, but you may have other things that could be of interest to them. They won't know about what else you can offer them unless you tell them. It may seem obvious but the simple things are often the most effective. Get your customers to take the blinkers off and see what else is available.

10. **Until further notice deals**

Create a sense of urgency and deadline by which to buy to receive a special deal. Most people love a good deal and can't resist. It is human nature to not want to feel as though we have missed out on something. A deadline forces a customer's hand and compels a decision to be made.

11.   Ask them to come back

This is linked to your communication strategy. Don't forget customers once they have purchased from you. Ask them to come back and purchase again by providing a reason to do so, which may be an incentive offer on their next purchase or an offer of a free trial. There are loads of things you can do here.

12.   Collect a database of potential clients

This is about building your mailing list for marketing purposes so that you can start the process of building trust and rapport over time until they get to a point where there is sufficient trust for a transaction to occur. Don't bombard subscribers with meaningless and pointless messages. They will soon tire of it and it will do more harm than good. Treating others as you would like and expect to be treated yourself is a good rule of thumb to follow.

13.   Increase your range

Don't be a one-trick pony. By understanding the needs of your clients, you can expand your range to include other products and services that you know your clients will be more inclined to want and need, thereby encouraging them to undertake more transactions with you.

14.   Plan future purchases

Help your clients plan for their future needs. Help them see beyond the short term and think about the medium to longer term. For example, if you are in a plumbing business help them plan their future boiler maintenance requirements.

15. **Special occasion cards**

This could mean birthdays, anniversaries, Christmas – basically any relevant special occasion to show that you care about your clients. Have a reminder system in place to manage and automate as much as possible for greatest efficiency.

16. **Direct mail/email regular offers**

Success here relates to staying in regular touch and providing attractive and compelling incentives that make your target clients stop and pay attention to what you are saying. Don't bombard or overwhelm them and definitely don't SPAM.

17. **Past customer events**

Invite past customers along to a cocktail party or product launch so that you can re-engage with them and show them why they should buy from you again. Be proactive.

18. **Always have stock**

We live in an instant gratification society. People generally want an instant solution. Also you can't sell something and cause a transaction to occur if you don't have stock available to sell. Don't give a customer a reason to look elsewhere by not being able to provide the product or service they are seeking at the time they are seeking it.

19. Contracts

Offer contracts that meet the needs of the client over an extended period of time beyond the initial transaction. For example, consider a time-based contract such as for a period of twelve months or perhaps offer service and maintenance contracts.

20. Product of the week

This one should be self-explanatory.

21. Increase product obsolescence/upgrades

The goal here is to compel clients to come back regularly to keep up with any product and service enhancements.

22. Accept trade-ins

Again, this is about making it easy for a customer to buy from you and tackling any obstacles that may prevent a sale from happening.

23. Increase credit level

Take a credit card for instance. If our limit is $3,000 and it is raised by the banks to $5,000, then we have an extra $2,000 to buy stuff with if we choose. By lifting the credit level, further spend is encouraged. Be careful with this one though, and ensure that the additional financial risk attached doesn't outweigh the benefits received. A balance must be struck.

24. Sell more consumables

Sell more things that are used and don't exist once consumed. Think about food. If you eat an apple, then that apple no longer exists so if you want another apple you need to buy another one. Or think about a printer; you need ink for the printer to work properly and ink runs out so you need to keep buying ink for the printer to work as you want and expect it to.

25. Offer big customers a shareholding in your company

This is certainly not for the faint-hearted. Give your big customers an aligned interest so that they always buy through you. They then have a vested interest in the success of your business.

JUST FOR FUN EXERCISE

STEP 1

I hope these ideas helped stimulate some thoughts on what you could do in your business. So I want you to think about your business specifically. Your task is to brainstorm five ideas for ways that will encourage more transactions to be made by your customers by 25% during the next year.

You should be asking yourself, "How can I improve the frequency with which customers or clients buy my products or services by 25% over the next year?" That means if currently a customer buys from you on average four times a year, then what can you do to increase this by one transaction to five transactions in the next twelve months?

Now, if you can't think of five ideas then you aren't thinking hard enough and need to try harder! I want you to be bold in your thinking. Be creative and have fun with it.

IDEA 1

IDEA 2

IDEA 3

IDEA 4

IDEA 5

STEP 2

Now I want you to give the five top ideas that you have brainstormed a mark out of 10 that reflects the likely effectiveness, the confidence you have to do it, the availability of resources to implement it and the likely results.

IDEA 1 _____ / 10

IDEA 2 _____ / 10

IDEA 3 _____ / 10

IDEA 4 _____ / 10

IDEA 5 _____ / 10

It's important that you do not move on from this chapter until you complete the ideas and rank them as instructed. All will make sense later in the book.

So, in this chapter we have covered the third of the five key focus areas. As with all the five key focus areas we are covering, this area by itself is yet another goldmine of opportunity, as most businesses never collect a database of their past customers, let alone write to them or call them and ask them to come back.

CHAPTER 9

Key Focus 4 –
Average sale value

NUMBER OF CUSTOMERS

x

Number of transactions (3)

x

Average sale value (4)

=

REVENUE

This is one area that at least some business owners do measure. Every product or service a business provides has a price associated with it, which represents what must be paid by a customer to buy a product or benefit from a specific service a business provides.

The price represents the sale value for that item. However, if a client buys more than one thing at the same time, then the sale value for that particular transaction is the sum total of all items purchased at that point. Think about your weekly grocery shopping. You typically buy more than one item when you do your food shopping but only one transaction happens for that visit to the supermarket.

The value of the transaction is worked out by adding up the individual prices of the groceries that are in your shopping trolley. It is the total amount you must pay to go home with everything you put in your trolley on that occasion.

For example, assume a customer buys the following items on a visit to a shop:

Item 1 sells for	$2.00 (A)
Item 2 sells for	$5.00 (B)
Item 3 sells for	$10.00 (C)
Item 4 sells for	$15.00 (D)
Item 5 sells for	$8.00 (E)
Total Sale Value =	$40.00 (A + B + C +D + E)

In this case, the total value of the transaction occurring is $40.00. This is the total amount that the customer must pay for this visit to the shop.

Once again, some customers will spend more with you and some will spend less each time they buy something from you. What you want to know is the average that customers spend with you in total each time.

Simply add up your total sales and then divide it by the number of transactions incurred in generating those sales.

For example, assume the following five transactions have happened in a set period:

Transaction 1	$40.00
Transaction 2	$60.00
Transaction 3	$100.00
Transaction 4	$125.00
Transaction 5	$75.00

Step 1: Add up the total value of the transactions, which in this case comes to $400.00.

Step 2: Identify the number of underlying transactions involved to generate this revenue, which in this case is five transactions.

Step 3: Divide the revenue figure by the number of transactions involved in generating that revenue. In this case there were five transactions involved, so $400 revenue divided by five transactions results in an average sale value of $80.00 per transaction in that set period.

That's how you arrive at the average sale value amount.

PRE-EXERCISE HEADS UP

I want you to think about your business as you read through the 25 ideas for improving the average sale value per transaction in your business that we are about to cover. Your task at the end of it will be to brainstorm five ideas for ways that you can improve the amount that your customers or clients spend with you each year by 25%. So simply bear this in mind as you read through the possible ideas over the coming pages.

There will be space after this section for you to write down the five ideas you have come up with that you think could help you improve your average sale value by 25% over the next year, so just have your thinking head fully engaged and on for now.

An important thing to note is that some of the ideas may not be applicable or relevant for your business, but that's okay. The ideas provided are designed to stimulate your thinking and some ideas may apply to more than one focus area.

25 ideas to help get you started

1. Increase your prices

This might seem a bit obvious so is easily overlooked, but by raising your prices you increase your average sale value. Customers will be paying you more for the same products or services every time they buy from you. Obviously, this isn't always an easy thing to do and there may be market forces at play that prevent you from doing it, especially if you operate within a competitive marketplace.

This is beneficial to a business provided the rise in prices, and resultant revenue, isn't offset by a reduction in transactions occurring. You will know if there is scope to raise prices or not but it is a really good place to start to improve your average sale value amounts.

2. Provide a checklist

Inform your customers what they should buy or show them what other people would typically buy when they have had the same need. Train your customers.

Imagine how grateful you would feel if, say, you wanted to start a new hobby and when you went into a hobby shop to enquire they presented you with a list of everything you would need to get started. This list might include things you didn't even know you needed. And guess what? Everything you needed you could buy in that shop, then and there. Do you think that might influence your decision to buy or not?

3. Up-sell

This involves suggesting a product or service that is one bracket higher than the one under consideration. Selling a higher-priced item means a higher sale value.

4. Stop discounting

Think about what discounting is. It is where you reduce the amount you charge for a product or service. If you stop doing it, then the amount you receive is higher.

5. Set and measure an average sale value target

How do you know what your average sale value is if you don't measure it? The very act of measuring something puts it in focus and creates a platform for future improvements. Setting targets focuses the attention of your team.

6. Sell with an either/or question

This is a clever one. It lets a customer think they have a choice but the end result is still a sale for your business. For example, would you like that delivered on Tuesday or Thursday? In this case, revenue from a delivery charge boosts the sale value for this transaction in either outcome.

7. Allow credit cards, debit cards and cheques

Make it as easy as possible for your customers to give you their money and to spend more than they have currently on them in cash!

8. Team incentives for bigger sales

Provide team incentives that encourage higher sale amounts. This is closely linked to setting targets and rewarding success. You may pay higher commissions on some items of higher value than you would on lower-priced transactions. Be creative with it but be sure that any rewards are aligned to the objectives of and a successful outcome for your business.

9. **Suggest the most expensive item first and down-sell as appropriate**

Show them a higher-priced item first, and then the one just a little more expensive than they originally had in mind will seem cheap.

10. **Allow payment terms or finance**

Let customers spend money they don't currently have. Help them spend more with you. Perhaps offer special arrangements on higher-priced items only and not lower-priced items, which encourages the customer to opt for higher-priced items to get the added benefit.

11. **Carry exclusive lines**

When you provide a product or service that a customer or client can't get elsewhere, there is more scope to be a price-setter because of the reduced competition. Also create a quality image so customers are more likely to pay a premium price for the quality you provide them!

12. **Charge for delivery, postage and packaging**

Most businesses that offer delivery and charge for postage and packaging charge a higher amount than it costs them to deliver the product. This could be an additional source of revenue for your business.

13. **Add perceived value**

This could be anything that you can provide at minimal cost but is seen as very valuable from a customer's perspective and they would be prepared to pay more to receive.

14. Build rapport and treat as special

Genuinely care about your customers and it will come back to you many times over.

15. Stock more high-priced ranges

If you introduce ranges that sell for more, then your average sale value will obviously increase with it – provided the higher-priced ranges sell of course. For service businesses, you may be able to introduce silver, gold and platinum levels of services at increasing pricing levels.

16. Sell service contracts

This involves selling something that complements what the client has purchased. This could include extended after-sales care contracts over a defined period.

17. Create bulk buy or package deals

Create tailored packages that contain items that a customer or client is seeking and perhaps give them a discount when buying more at the same time.

18. Give a gift with minimum purchase

Give customers something that has a high-perceived value but costs you very little when they spend over a specified amount with your business. It may take the form of free delivery when a customer spends a certain amount with you, as we frequently see on many e-commerce websites these days.

19.   Educate on value – not price

Avoid having to compete on price wherever possible as it usually ends up involving having to discount or lower prices, which is the complete opposite to the objective of this exercise which is to increase the average sale value. Help your clients to understand why they should buy from you, and not another business, and explain the reasons why the price of an item represents real value to them.

20.   Ask people to buy some more and cross-sell

Think about McDonalds again and what they do when you order a burger. They say, "Would you like fries with that?" They ask you to buy more. Be creative about ways you can use this same principle in your business. Point out special offers that may be of interest. Encourage impulse buys where possible also. Remember, there is no harm in asking the question and generally the worst someone can say is "no thanks."

21.   Buy one get one free offers

A variation of this theme may be four for the price of three promotions. We see them all the time in supermarkets. Be careful though, you must have sufficient profit margins to justify such a strategy or it could be costly to your business. You must know your numbers to do this. Any deals that involve effectively discounting for higher levels of volume must be profit margin dependent but can be excellent for encouraging greater volume if the margins allow.

22. Charge consulting fees

What are you currently doing for free for your clients that you can begin charging them for which is seen as valuable from their perspective?

23. Sell extra warranty or insurance

This is predicated on giving clients added peace of mind but at the same time being a very valuable source of revenue for your business at very little cost.

24. Customer incentives for bigger purchases

Provide customers with added incentives that encourage them to make bigger purchases with you. This can take many forms but, as has been mentioned previously, the key is to focus on providing incentives that have a high perceived value in the eyes of the customer but cost you very little to provide in monetary terms. Get it right and it is a winning formula.

25. Have a minimum value order amount

You set the minimum order value for someone to be able to order from you. We frequently see it used in the case of the acceptance of credit and debit cards, where you have to spend a certain amount before you can pay with them.

JUST FOR FUN EXERCISE

STEP 1

I hope the ideas helped stimulate some thoughts on what you could do in your business. So I want you to think about your business specifically. Your task is to brainstorm five ideas for ways that you can encourage and increase the total sale value amount every time your customers or clients buy from you by 25% over the next year.

You should be asking yourself, "How could I get my customers or clients to spend 25% more on products or services every time they transact with me over the next year?" That means if currently a customer spends on average $100 every time they buy from you, what can you do to increase this by $25 to $125 in the next year?

Now, if you can't think of five ideas then you aren't thinking hard enough and need to try harder! I want you to be bold in your thinking. Be creative and have fun with it.

IDEA 1

_____

_____

_____

IDEA 2

_____

_____

_____

IDEA 3
_____

_____

_____

IDEA 4
_____

_____

_____

IDEA 5
_____

_____

_____

STEP 2

Now I want you to give the five top ideas that you have brainstormed a mark out of 10 that reflects the likely effectiveness, the confidence you have to do it, the availability of resources to implement it and the likely results.

IDEA 1 _____ / 10

IDEA 2 _____ / 10

IDEA 3 _____ / 10

IDEA 4 _____ / 10

IDEA 5 _____ / 10

It's important that you do not move on from this chapter until you complete the ideas and rank them as instructed. All will make sense later in the book, I promise!

So, in this chapter we have covered the fourth of the five key focus areas. It is the combination of the two factors we covered in this chapter and the preceding chapter together with the 'number of customers' result that determines the revenue amount for a set period of time.

Remember that the revenue amount is a RESULT, which can't be influenced directly. This result can only be changed by focusing on what influences the result, which are the four key focus areas we have covered so far.

You need to multiply the total number of customers you dealt with by the number of times they came back on average, and then by the average amount they spent with you each time. That's your revenue.

Put simply:

NUMBER OF CUSTOMERS
x
Number of transactions (3)
x
Average sale value (4)
=
REVENUE

This is another area most business owners will know the answer to, but they most probably have no real idea how they got to it. Of course, you want more of it, but you can't simply get more *revenue!* However...

What you can encourage is more transactions and a higher average sale value from the total number of customers or clients you deal with.

Making sense? It's a subtle but important difference.

CHAPTER 10

Key Focus 5 – Margins

REVENUE

x

Margin (5)

=

PROFIT

Margins represent the percentage of each and every sale that's profit. In other words, if you sold something for $100 and $25 was profit, then you've got a 25% margin.

In Chapter 5 we introduced the concept of gross profit margin and net profit margin. We said that *gross profit* is the difference between the selling price of a product or service and the *direct* costs taken to produce that product or service. These direct costs are also known as *variable costs.*

Variable costs are those costs that tend to fluctuate with the level of sales. They include, but are not limited to, such things as direct labour, raw materials, sales commissions and delivery expenses. They represent the *costs of the goods sold.*

At a whole business level, gross profit is the difference between the sum of all the revenue generated from all sources and the sum of all the variable costs or direct costs of the goods sold to generate that revenue. It doesn't take into account the overheads or fixed costs of the business at this level. The *gross profit margin* expresses the gross profit amount as a percentage of revenue.

We then went on to explore *net profit*, the next layer down. We showed that it is the residual profit after all the fixed costs or overheads of the business have been deducted.

Fixed costs are those costs that do not tend to fluctuate with the level of sales. They include, but are not limited to, such things as rent, equipment leases, insurance, interest on borrowed funds, business taxes and administrative salaries.

The *net profit margin* expresses the net profit amount as a percentage of revenue. It is the net profit margin that we are most interested in here; at the end of the day that is what's left for you after all costs including taxes have been deducted. It represents the chocolate left in the box for you to enjoy yourself. The higher your net profit, the more chocolates you have to enjoy!

At a very basic level, margins can be influenced in two ways:

1.   Increasing prices at a greater rate than the associated costs of providing that product or service.
2.   Reducing your costs at a rate that is greater than any reduction in prices.

Let's apply three scenarios to extend the example we used back in Chapter 5, which was based on the following summary information:

Total Revenue	$350,000	(A)
Total costs of good sold	$200,000	(B)
Gross profit	$150,000	C (A-B)
Total fixed costs/overheads	$80,000	(D)
Net profit	$70,000	E (C-D)
Net Profit Margin	20.0%	F (E/A x 100)

Scenario 1

You decide to put all your prices up by 10% only. There is no impact on your costs by taking this action. This means that your revenue figure would increase by $35,000 (A x 10%) to $385,000. Let's see the impact this would have on your net profit amount and margin.

Total Revenue	$385,000
Total costs of good sold	$200,000
Gross profit	$185,000
Total fixed costs/overheads	$80,000
Net profit	$105,000
Net Profit Margin	27.3%

This results in an increase in your net profit margin from 20.0% to 27.3%, which is 7.3 whole percentage points and represents a 36.4% (7.3% divided by 20%) improvement. A result you should be happy with.

Scenario 2

You manage to negotiate better terms with your suppliers, which results in a 20% reduction in your costs of goods sold. There is no impact on your revenue by achieving these savings. This means that your costs of goods sold figure would decrease by $40,000 (B x 20%) to $160,000. Let's see the impact this would have on your net profit amount and margin.

Total Revenue	$350,000
Total costs of good sold	$160,000
Gross profit	$190,000

Total fixed costs/overheads $80,000
Net profit $110,000

Net Profit Margin   31.4%

This results in an increase in your net profit margin from 20.0% to 31.4%, which is 11.4 percentage points and represents a 57.1% (11.4% divided by 20%) improvement. Surely this result would make you even happier.

Scenario 3

Now let's look at the impact if you manage to increase your prices by 10% as in Scenario 1 and you also manage to negotiate better terms with your suppliers resulting in a 20% reduction in your costs of goods sold, as illustrated in Scenario 2.

This means that your revenue figure would increase by $35,000 (A x 10%) to $385,000 and that your costs of goods sold figure would decrease by $40,000 (B x 20%) to $160,000. Let's see the impact this would have on your net profit amount and margin.

Total Revenue	$385,000
Total costs of good sold	$160,000
Gross profit	$225,000
Total fixed costs/overheads	$80,000
Net profit	$145,000
Net Profit Margin	37.7%

This results in an increase in your net profit margin from 20.0% to 37.7%, which is 17.7 percentage points and represents an 88.3% (17.7% divided by 20%) improvement. Let's look at what this means to the money going into your pocket.

Previously, you were left with $20.00 in every $100 of revenue being generated by your business. After completing the two initiatives to improve your margins, you are now walking away with $37.70 in every $100 of revenue being generated. That's **an extra $17.70** in every $100 of revenue for not doing anything extra in providing the underlying product or service. That extra profit is better off in your pocket than someone else's pocket, is it not?

Now that should be something to get excited about. If it doesn't give you enough incentive to start looking at your margins more closely, I don't know what will!

PRE-EXERCISE HEADS UP

As this is such a vital focus area, I am going to share with you some extra ideas to help get you started, more than I did for the other focus areas. I want you to think about your business as you read through the 35 ideas for improving margins in your business that we are about to cover. Your task at the end of it will be to brainstorm five ideas for ways that you can improve your overall net profit margin by 25% during the next year. So simply bear this in mind as you read through the possible ideas over the coming pages.

There will be space after this section for you to write down the five ideas you have come up with that you think could help you improve your overall net profit margin by 25% over the next year, so just have your thinking head fully engaged and on for now.

An important thing to note is that some of the ideas may not be applicable or relevant for your business, but that's okay. The ideas provided are designed to stimulate your thinking and some ideas may apply to more than one focus area.

35 ideas to help get you started

1. Increase your prices

We saw the potential impact of this in Scenario 1. The key here is to make sure any price increases are greater than any increase in the underlying costs for providing that product or service, so that it has a positive impact on the margins being made. How long has it been since you looked at your prices? When was the last time you raised them?

Obviously, the ability to increase prices will be dependent on the type of business you operate and the marketplace you operate in. A business in a competitive marketplace is less likely to be able to increase prices easily than a business that has differentiated itself from its competition.

2. Streamline your operations

Reduce unnecessary management. Systemise the routine, humanise the exceptions. It's all about becoming more efficient. Reduce duplication where possible and automate as much as possible. Make sure you are taking advantage of any technological advancements that are relevant for your business that can help you provide your products and services more efficiently, which generally translates into lower costs.

3.   Know your actual costs

You can't improve what you don't know. Know what things cost and make sure you include everything. Don't leave any costs out. To better manage the results you need to have access to regular management information on this area, which should be produced frequently. Stay on top of the numbers. Monitor performance regularly, always keeping your profit in focus!

4.   Join or start a buying group

Team up with other businesses that buy the same resources as you. It is called economy of scale and is based on the principle that the bigger the volume, the better the deal. The objective here is to achieve cost savings through co-operating with other businesses to facilitate bulk purchasing.

5.   Pay with cash rather than loan interest

Interest on loans and overdrafts is a cost to a business so therefore reduces your margins. Don't pay with debt if you don't need to, especially if you have cash available to pay instead. It's not always possible to do this but with careful management of your cash flow, the need for using such costly things as factoring and invoice discounting can usually be eliminated.

6.   Change your advisers.

Look at what you are spending on advisers each year. You might want to consider changing the professionals you work with. This may lead to cost savings when switching and result in improved arrangements that better meet your needs and expectations. If appropriate, massive savings can be made by switching, as professionals compete to win your new custom. However, make sure you seek out professionals who understand and are supportive of your future plans.

7.   **Keep overheads to a minimum**

Don't take on any unnecessary cost commitments that aren't linked to revenue generation activities. Stay lean and keep your overheads under control.

8.   **Stop running ads that don't work**

Any marketing that isn't working is a cost. Remember, as we covered previously, marketing should be seen as an investment. You want to keep the good investments and cut your losses on the bad investments. Don't keep doing something just because you have always done it that way. It's a complete waste of time and money. Every $1 you waste on unnecessary expenditure is $1 less in your pocket. This is a good principle to always keep in mind.

9.   **Buy only what you need**

Don't have excess supplies hanging around unnecessarily. Have a system in place to control the purchases of your team. This could be done by only allowing your team to buy with an authorised purchase order. Any money tied up in unnecessary supplies is money that isn't working for you to help generate more revenue.

10. **Reduce 30-day terms to 7 days**

The aim of the game is to get the money due to your business in as quickly as possible so you can redeploy it into activities that support revenue generation. Remember, a profit isn't real until it is received as cash in your bank account. Cash is king.

Consider providing your customers with incentives that encourage early payments, such as a discount for early payment. The flip of this is that you want to delay as much as possible any cash outflows from the business by negotiating extended payment terms with your suppliers.

11. **Take stock on consignment**

This means that you have the stock you need on hand to sell, but you only pay for it when it is sold.

12. **Re-finance**

Look at all of your loans, credit cards and any type of finance facility you utilise. Shop around for a better deal to reduce your interest cost or payment amounts to help with cash flow. Look to negotiate lower payments but over a longer time horizon. Any interest or fees you can save will positively impact your margins.

13. **Sell only fast-moving stock**

Stock that sits idle on the shelf costs you money. By selling only fast-moving stock, you reduce the holding costs associated with having that stock on hand. The quicker you can turn over your stock, the more scope you have to buy more and repeat the cycle in a given period. Idle stock stops you from doing this. Why stock something that your customers don't want to buy?

14. Reduce or eliminate taxation expense

Remember, tax is a cost to your business and it can represent a large chunk of your profit. It can be as much as 40% of your profit. Effective tax planning is a key ingredient to improving your margins.

Don't misunderstand what I'm saying here; I'm not advocating tax avoidance. What I am saying is that there are legitimate and legal ways of minimising the amount of tax you need to pay and to ignore this area when trying to achieve savings is foolish, in my opinion. Get good tax planning advice from an expert in this area such as a tax accountant.

15. Buy in bulk, pay and receive over time

This is where you agree to buy a bigger volume from a supplier on better terms, so you benefit from economies of scale but you receive the goods or services over an extended period of time as you need them and only pay for them as you use or sell the underlying goods or services.

The upside in such an arrangement, especially when purchasing stock, is that the holding costs of the stock remain with the supplier and are not transferred to you. Your cash flow will thank you also for this arrangement. The supplier is happy because they are guaranteed a certain volume of sales over a specified period time. Win/win, everyone's happy!

16.   Reduce all costs by 10%

Undertake a business-wide campaign to cut all costs by 10% or whatever percentage reduction you are seeking. Perhaps consider incentivising and rewarding your team for achieving whatever cost reduction target you set.

17.   Set monthly expenditure budgets

Put limits on what can be spent each month. This is a fundamental cost-controlling tool. It focuses the mind and the decisions that follow in deciding how best to allocate a limited resource to meet the desired objectives.

Measure everything – unless you measure it, the true cost is hard to know. You also need a base from which to benchmark improvements.

18.   Decrease range

Bigger isn't always better. Focus on the products or services that are the most profitable for you. Get rid of those with lower margins if you can.

19.   Better negotiation skills

This is all about being better at negotiating such things as employment agreements, rents, supplier terms, professional fees and other fixed expenses. Remember, every $1 you save is $1 you put back into your pocket. Every $1 counts.

20. Sell more big-margin goods/services

If you sell more products or services with a higher profit margin than those products or services with a lower profit margin, then your overall profit margin will improve. Introduce more high-margin goods and services wherever you can and sell more of them.

21. Do it right the first time

The costs of re-work in business can be huge and are often ignored and overlooked. By doing it once and doing it properly, you avoid the costs associated with re-works, which can be disproportionate to the revenue received.

22. Charge for a finance facility

Find ways of charging for things that you are not currently charging for but you do anyway, so there is minimal incremental cost to your business. Many businesses now charge late payment fees or interest on late payments. Banks charge fees for overdraft facilities so why can't you consider something similar for any finance facilities you may offer your customers or clients?

23. Reduce team size

Not always an easy thing to do. But the process in becoming more efficient and streamlined is removing the elements that are redundant and not needed. This can mean people. Just be sure to make any changes in this area in the proper way.

24.   Repackage smaller

Look at your packaging. Is there any waste involved? Are you over-packaging? Find ways of achieving the same result with less packaging, which means less cost. Both the environment and your bottom line will thank you for it.

25.   Get your bills checked

Just because a utility bill shows an amount doesn't necessarily mean it is correct. Can you be sure that you are even on the right tariff? Make sure you are not overpaying for your utilities.

26.   Get rid of difficult or less profitable customers

Sack your less profitable customers. You will find that your less profitable customers will usually provide you with the most headaches. It is the old 80/20 principle, which in this case means that 20% of your customers constitute 80% of your headaches.

Not only will doing this make your life easier, it will free up the time and resources required to focus on seeking out more profitable customers.

27.   Sell your own label or an exclusive label

Avoid paying a premium price for someone else's brand when you can create something yourself and cut out the middlemen that eat into your profits at every step of the way. Exclusive lines tend to be higher margin in nature, and if the exclusive line can be sold at a premium price then that adds to the benefits of pursuing such a strategy.

28. Keep an accurate database

This avoids unnecessary waste when sending out marketing material. The more accurate your database, the higher your return on marketing is likely to be when undertaking any marketing initiatives and the less wastage there will be.

29. Sell via the internet

An e-commerce website replaces, in many instances, the need for a physical shop with the huge associated costs of having a physical location. This usually translates into lower overheads with the added benefit of having greater geographical reach, as the internet is global and borderless.

30. Recycle

This is about being savvy in the use and allocation of your business resources. Consider things that you can use more than once or for a different purpose after it has been used for its primary purpose. Not only can it improve your bottom line but the environment will be grateful to you as well.

31. Manufacture it yourself

Sometimes it is more cost-effective to make a product yourself rather than buy it from other suppliers who have their own profit margin and mark-up included in the price you pay. This also gives you more control of the output.

32. Promote idle time

This is about making the best use of quiet times. Offer special deals in your less busy times so that your staff aren't left sitting idle. Remember, employees are resources that generally must be paid for irrespective of how busy the business is. Make the most of resources so that you get maximum return on your investment.

33. Rent idle space

Excess space that you don't need or aren't currently using may be able to be sub-let. Obviously there are rules and restrictions that may apply but if this is possible it could turn idle space into a source of additional revenue for your business. Could you consider downsizing to a smaller office or outlet?

34. Employ people in-house

For an identified skill set, it is generally more cost-effective to employ that resource in-house than continue to pay inflated agency or consulting fees. The primary reason is that agencies and consultants need to charge a premium over what the person is actually being paid to cover their overheads and make a profit. There are other benefits to bringing key skills in-house such as greater control and flexibility.

35. Outsource

For non-essential operational functions, it is often cheaper to outsource those functions to third party providers who, because of their size and scale, can fulfil that function more cheaply than you could ever do yourself.

Like anything, there are benefits and pitfalls to look out for. Approach this whole area with your eyes wide open and make sure expectations are clear and processes well documented. If done properly, however, this area could generate significant cost savings for your business.

JUST FOR FUN EXERCISE

STEP 1

I hope the ideas helped stimulate some thoughts on what you could do in your business. So I want you to think about your business specifically. Your task is to brainstorm five ideas for ways that you can improve your overall net profit margin by 25% during the next year.

You should be asking yourself, "What can I do to improve or how can my business be restructured in a way that results in more revenue with less cost that yields a 25% improvement in my net profit margin over the next year?" That means if currently your net profit margin is 20%, how can you improve that to 25% in the next year?

Now, if you can't think of five ideas then you aren't thinking hard enough and need to try harder! I want you to be bold in your thinking. Be creative and have fun with it.

IDEA 1
_____

_____

_____

_____

IDEA 2
_____

_____

_____

_____

IDEA 3
_____

_____

_____

_____

IDEA 4
_____

_____

_____

_____

IDEA 5
_____

_____

_____

_____

STEP 2

Now I want you to give the five top ideas that you have brainstormed a mark out of 10 that reflects the likely effectiveness, the confidence you have to do it, the availability of resources to implement it and the likely results.

IDEA 1 _____ / 10

IDEA 2 _____ / 10

IDEA 3 _____ / 10

IDEA 4 _____ / 10

IDEA 5 _____ / 10

It's important that you do not move on from this chapter until you complete the ideas and rank them as instructed. All will make sense in the next chapter.

So, in this chapter we have covered the fifth and final of the five key focus areas, this being margin which determines the profit being made after all costs have been deducted.

Remember that the profit amount is a RESULT, which can't be influenced directly. This result can only be changed by focusing on what influences the result, which are the five key focus areas we have covered so far.

Every business owner wants more profit, not realising that *they can't simply just get more profit*, but they can earn greater margins on the revenue they are generating to improve the amount of profit that results.

Put simply:

REVENUE
x
Margin (5)
=
PROFIT

And that's it. This Profit Accelerator Formula can be applied to any business on earth!

By simply breaking down your business and marketing efforts into these five key focus areas and understanding how each affects the other, you're halfway there –and way ahead of 90% of businesses out there.

The true power of combining the power of each of the five key focus areas we are covering in this book is yet to come and all will be revealed in the next chapter. Prepare to get really excited!

CHAPTER 11

The power of Profit Accelerator Formula

Over the past five chapters you have been introduced to the five key focus areas to transform the profits of your business. Before I show you the power of what you have in your hands right now, let's just take a breather and go through a summary of what we have covered.

KEY FOCUS AREA 1 – Number of leads

This is the total number of potential buyers that you have contacted or that contacted you last year – also known as prospects or potentials.

KEY FOCUS AREA 2 – Conversion rate

Your conversion rate is the percentage of people who did actually buy from you as opposed to those who could have bought. For example, if you had ten people walk through your store today and you sold to only three of them, you'd have a conversion rate of three out of ten, or 30%.

KEY FOCUS AREA 3 – Number of transactions

Some of your customers or clients will buy from you weekly, others monthly, others on the odd occasion and others just once in a lifetime. What you want to know now is the average – not your best and not your worst, but the average number of times one of your customers buys from you in a year.

KEY FOCUS AREA 4 – Average sale value

Every product or service a business provides has a price associated which represents what must be paid by a customer to buy it. The price represents the sale value for that item. However, if a client buys more than one thing at the same time, then the sale value for that particular transaction is the sum total of all items purchased at that point.

KEY FOCUS AREA 5 - Margins

Margins represent the percentage of each and every sale that's profit. In other words, if you sold something for $100 and $25 was profit, then you've got a 25% margin. Remember, this is after **all costs** are taken out.

Profit Accelerator Formula

Each of the five key focus areas interacts as follows:

Number of Leads (1)
x
Conversion Rate (2)
=
NUMBER OF CUSTOMERS
x
Number of Transactions (3)
x
Average Sale Value (4)
=
REVENUE
x
Margin (5)
=
PROFIT

Now let's look at a case study where I demonstrate to you how small changes to each of these focus areas can transform the profits of your business.

John and Jenny run a service business. They are passionate about their business but by their own admission have neglected the numbers side of the business because of fear and lack of confidence in this area. They have largely adopted the typical ostrich mentality and have their heads in the sand when it comes to financial matters. They were under the mistaken belief that their accountant was looking after this part of the business for them, but in reality the accountant was only engaged to do the very basics that ensure the statutory reporting obligations for their business are met.

The business has limped along and both John and Jenny are extremely busy doing what they do but aren't making any money to reflect the effort they are putting in. They are fed up and at the end of their tether because their employees are earning more than they do without any of the levels of stress and worry they experience. Something had to give, as they couldn't keep on at that pace. They recognised they needed help on the numbers side of their business, and they could no longer ignore it. They took back control of their own destiny and became accountable to themselves in doing what it takes to improve the situation and take their business to the next level in generating more profits.

The first 90 days were spent sorting through everything that had been ignored or put in the 'too hard' basket. They found that when supported through this process it wasn't nearly as scary as they expected it to be. They felt reassured that they were working with someone to hold their hand through the process.

During this 90-day period, one of the objectives was to identify the relevant values for each of the five key focus areas of the Profit Accelerator Formula. Some were easier to identify than others, as they were able to extract data from their accounting package with some help. They found that the trickiest ones to work out were their number of leads and the conversion rate, so they set up a system to begin tracking them. At the end of the 90 days they had enough information to estimate with some confidence the values they needed. They were reassured to hear that it isn't about perfection; it is about moving forward one step at a time. The information they had gathered meant that they were further ahead than they were if they hadn't completed the tracking exercise. That was progress and they felt better for it.

At the end of that 90-day period, they were able to break their last annual results down into the following components of the Profit Accelerator Formula:

Number of leads per year	1,000
Conversion rate	20%
Number of transactions	4
Average Sale Value	$500
Margin	20%

Profit accelerator formula applied

Number of Leads (1)	1,000
x	
Conversion Rate (2)	20%
=	
NUMBER OF CUSTOMERS	**200**
x	
Number of Transactions (3)	4
x	
Average Sale Value (4)	$500
=	
REVENUE	**$400,000**
x	
Margin (5)	20%
=	
PROFIT	**$80,000**

This meant that John and Jenny's business at that point had 200 customers for the year and produced revenue of $400,000. This resulted in a profit, after all costs have been deducted, of $80,000.

Make sense?

John and Jenny felt really pleased to reach this point and became really excited when they were shown the following three different scenarios.

Scenario 1:   *Improve each key focus area by 10%*
Scenario 2:   *Improve each key focus area by 15%*
Scenario 3:   *And JUST FOR FUN improve each key focus area by 25%*

Scenario 1: Improve each key focus area by 10%

The impact of improving each of the key focus areas by a modest 10% would be the following:

Number of leads per year	1,000 to 1,100
Conversion rate	20% to 22%
Number of transactions	4.0 to 4.4
Average Sale Value	$500 to $550
Margin	20% to 22%

Profit Accelerator Formula applied

Number of Leads (1)	1,100
x	
Conversion Rate (2)	22%
=	
NUMBER OF CUSTOMERS	242
x	
Number of Transactions (3)	4.4
x	
Average Sale Value (4)	$550
=	
REVENUE	**$585,640**
x	
Margin (5)	22%
=	
PROFIT	**$128,841**

Now let's look at what this would mean for John and Jenny's business. A modest 10% improvement in each of the key focus areas would mean the following results:

- Their number of customers increasing by 42, from 200 to 242, which is a 21.0% improvement
- Total revenue increasing by $185,640, from $400,000 to $585,640, which is a massive 46.4% improvement
- Net profit increasing by $48,841, from $80,000 to $128,841, which is a staggering 61.1% improvement

Scenario 2: Improve each key focus area by 15%

The impact of improving each of the key focus areas by a higher but still modest 15% would be the following:

Number of leads per year	1,000 to 1,150
Conversion rate	20% to 23%
Number of transactions	4.0 to 4.6
Average Sale Value	$500 to $575
Margin	20% to 23%

Profit Accelerator Formula applied

Number of Leads (1)	1,150
x	
Conversion Rate (2)	23%
=	
NUMBER OF CUSTOMERS	**265**
x	
Number of Transactions (3)	4.6
x	
Average Sale Value (4)	$575
=	
REVENUE	**$700,925**
x	
Margin (5)	23%
=	
PROFIT	**$161,213**

Now let's look at what this would mean for John and Jenny's business. A higher but still modest 15% improvement in each of the key focus areas would mean the following results:

- Their number of customers increasing by 65, from 200 to 265, which is a 32.5% improvement
- Total revenue increasing by $300,925, from $400,000 to $700,925, which is a massive 75.2% improvement
- Net profit increasing by $81,213, from $80,000 to $161,213, which is a staggering 101.5% improvement. **That's more than a doubling of their profits!**

By this point, John and Jenny were getting really excited. They were starting to see how by neglecting the numbers they were neglecting their business. This resulted in the business underperforming and not fulfilling the potential they knew it had.

Just for fun, they undertook the very exercise that you have been asked to do in this book. I said completing the exercises would be important! They brainstormed loads of ideas on how they could improve each of the five key focus areas by 25% during the next year and settled on one strategy for each focus area that they were very confident was not only achievable, but within their capacity to deliver. They were waiting on the edge of their seats to find out what the impact would be on their bottom-line profit if successful.

Now, if you have done all of the exercises at the end of the focus area chapters, then you should have at least five ideas for strategies for each of the key focus areas that you are confident could deliver the 25% improvement sought for each area in the next year. This means you should have 25 ideas in total to choose from.

If you have really thought about and fully completed the exercises you should have a real sense that improvements at this level are possible, achievable and that you can do it. After all, there is absolutely nothing to lose by embracing the exercises and trying the new ideas. Your business won't be any worse off than it is for doing so, but the results could be truly transformational.

Let's find out just how transformational the ideas from the 'just for fun' exercises could be. Are you ready? It's time for you to get very excited, so brace yourself!

Scenario 3: Improve each key focus area by 25%

The impact of improving each of the key focus areas by an even higher but still achievable 25% would be the following:

Number of leads per year	1,000 to 1,250
Conversion rate	20% to 25%
Number of transactions	4.0 to 5.0
Average Sale Value	$500 to $625
Margin	20% to 25%

Profit accelerator formula applied

Number of Leads (1)	1,250
x	
Conversion Rate (2)	25%
=	
NUMBER OF CUSTOMERS	**313**
x	
Number of Transactions (3)	5.0
x	
Average Sale Value (4)	$625
=	
REVENUE	**$978,125**
x	
Margin (5)	25%
=	
PROFIT	**$244,531**

Now let's look at what this would mean for John and Jenny's business. An even higher but still achievable 25% improvement in each of the key focus areas would mean the following results:

- Their number of customers increasing by 113, from 200 to 313, which is a 56.5% improvement
- Total revenue increasing by $578,125, from $400,000 to $978,125, which is a massive 144.5% improvement
- Net profit increasing by $164,531, from $80,000 to $244,531, which is a mind-blowing 205.7% improvement. **That's more than a tripling of their profits!**

Now if that isn't enough to get you excited and interested in your numbers, I don't know what will! If you love and take care of your numbers, your business will love and take care of you back!

Just take a moment or two to really think about it and imagine just how good it will feel to receive a dividend cheque for three times the amount you have ever received before from your business, or a bank account that has three times as much money in it. Imagine it as if it is real and happening right NOW.

How do you feel? Do you feel proud? Do you feel energised? Do you feel richer? Do you feel invincible? Would you make any changes to your lifestyle? Would you do anything differently?

Small improvements to the five key focus areas we have covered in detail can result in dramatic changes to the bottom-line profits of your business. The right detail does definitely matter in that incremental smaller changes can transform the profits of your business.

By simply breaking down your business and marketing efforts into these five key focus areas and understanding how each affects the other, you're halfway there –and way ahead of 90% of businesses out there.

Get excited. Get very excited by this! What an opportunity you have before you to take back control of your business and its finances and take it to the next level of profitability that you know deep down it can reach. Remember, you don't have to necessarily do everything at once. Don't take on so much that it overwhelms you. Take it at your own pace. As long as you are moving forward that's all that counts. Take just one step at a time.

In the final chapter, I'll run through a 10-step blueprint you can use to get started today and we will recap on the key learning points from the journey we have shared through the course of this book.

CHAPTER 12

10-step blueprint and closing remarks

Well done on sticking with me this far. Hopefully you are feeling really excited about the potential opportunity that lies ahead in applying the Profit Accelerator Formula in your business. However, you are probably wondering how to go about doing it, so I have put together a 10-step blueprint to help you get started.

Step 1

Being clear on why you are doing what you do

In life we generally do everything for a reason. It is so important that you understand the reason you are in business. It will be a source of motivation, energy and commitment when you encounter more difficult patches. You must be clear on what you are trying to achieve with your business and why it is important to you.

We have to make choices every single day in business; being clear on your 'why' will help focus your attention on making the right choices that support where you are heading and will help you to filter out the opportunities or distractions along the way.

I shared with you my 'why' which is '*I truly believe that there is tremendous power at the intersection of entrepreneurialism and numeracy*'. I use this as my guiding principle in whatever I do in my business. I only look at introducing products and services that are aligned with my 'why'. Focus brings clarity and clarity brings better results.

Step 2

Get your financial records in order

If your accounts are in a state of disarray, you must take action and get them cleaned up and sorted out. If you can't do it yourself then get a resource to help you. Remember, there are rules, laws and obligations around keeping up-to-date and accurate financial records for your business, which include filing all relevant returns accurately and on time. Failure to do so risks huge fines and maybe even imprisonment. It is a very serious issue that must be dealt with so you must stop being an ostrich and remove your head from the sand immediately.

Apart from this very important reason, we need to identify a firm base from which to move forward and be able to work with the information to identify the relevant figures to use in the Profit Accelerator Formula. Any skeletons in the cupboard must be uncovered and dealt with.

How can you improve something if you don't know what it is to start with?

STEP 3

Information gathering

For each of the five key focus areas take your last set of annual accounts and break the results down into the five key focus areas of the Profit Accelerator Formula we have covered:

Number of leads

- Conversion rate
- Number of transactions
- Average sale value
- Margins

Number of leads

You may already have a customer relationship management (CRM) system that you use to track this information, from which you can simply extract the information. It's okay if you don't, you can do what John and Jenny did as they didn't have such a system in place and start tracking all of your leads over a 90-day period. Keep track of it on a simple spreadsheet or even in a notebook. You are seeking an indication from this exercise which will form a benchmark from which to improve. You need a starting point, though.

If you don't already have a system in place to capture this information, there are many inexpensive off-the-shelf software packages that you can buy to help in this area. These software and Cloud solutions can have either simple or more advanced functionality. Find the right package that works for you and is aligned to the needs of your customers and business.

Asking a simple question like "How did you hear about us?" can provide valuable insight into where best to target your activities moving forward.

Conversion rate

If you aren't currently tracking your conversion rate, you need to start doing so. It's okay if you're not, we can work backwards to identify what it is by looking at your **number of active customers** in a 12-month period and dividing that by your total number of leads identified in the first part of this step. Remember, the goal here is to have a starting point.

Number of transactions

This figure will usually come from your accounts. It is basically the number of invoices you have produced and sent out in that year.

Average sale value

This figure can be worked out by working backwards; also by taking the total revenue figure for the year and dividing it by the number of transactions (i.e. number of invoices produced and sent out for your products or services).

Margins

You calculate this by taking the net profit figure from the last set of annual accounts we are using for this exercise, which is usually at the bottom of the Profit and Loss statement, and dividing it by the total revenue as shown on the same report.

You will recall from what we have covered that margins represent the percentage of each and every sale that's profit. In other words, if you sold something for $100 and $25 was profit, then you've got a 25% margin. Remember, though, that this is after **all costs** are taken out.

STEP 4

Product or service profit check

You need to list all of the products and services you provide and work through each one to determine whether you are making money or not on that product or service. The reason for doing this is that it makes absolutely no sense to promote and seek greater volumes of sales for something that makes you very little or no money.

Without addressing the profitability issue for that product or service first, you are only making the problem worse when greater volumes are involved.

To do this exercise, you need to compare the price you are charging against all of the costs associated with providing that product or service at a gross profit level. Go back and re-read Chapter 5 if you need to remind yourself about the principles involved here.

The aim is to make sure that the revenue being received for each of your products or services is more than the costs being incurred, with sufficient left over at a gross profit level to contribute towards your fixed costs or overheads.

Remember, your gross profit represents the speed and ability of your business to cover its fixed costs and overheads and have something left over after all costs have been covered. The more gross profit you can generate, the quicker you can pay for your overheads and have something left over for you to enjoy, i.e. the net profit.

Get your house in order first on the profitability of your products and services before doing anything else. Make changes accordingly, based on the findings of this review. Again, if you don't feel confident enough to do this exercise yourself then get the help you need to complete the task.

STEP 5

Set the improvement targets

By this point you should have enough information to be able to identify all of the figures required for the Profit Accelerator Formula, which will form the foundation and base from which you will benchmark all your future improvements.

You will also have looked carefully at the profitability of each of your products and services and made changes where appropriate and necessary to ensure you are maximising the gross profit amount for each of them.

You now need to set the targets for improvement for each key focus area. I have put together a tool to help you do this so it should make your life much easier. Simply go to my website www.profitrocketbook.com/profittool and follow the instructions to download the tool for free.

The simple tool I have created enables you to enter different percentage improvement amounts for each key focus area and it will show you what the target will be to achieve that result for each specific focus area. It also shows you the combined impact of all of the improvements. It will make more sense when you see it, so I suggest you download it as soon as you can.

Remember, as we covered in Chapter 5 you want the targets you set to be SMART targets.

STEP 6

Using the ideas from the 'just for fun' exercises

Take the top three ideas from each key focus area that you brainstormed at the conclusion of the relevant chapter, the ones you gave the highest marks out of ten. Look into each of those ideas more closely, research where you have to, identify the resources you will need to do it, and write down what you will need to do to make it happen.

The aim is to emerge with **at least one initiative** for each area. Of course, you can have more than one initiative on the go at the same time if you can handle it, but I would suggest for starters that you stick with one initiative for each focus area for which you can carefully track and monitor the results.

The difficulty with having multiple strategies running at the same time, especially when it comes to marketing, is that unless a system is in place to carefully track the results, it can be difficult to know what has worked and what hasn't. It's like deciding to do a detox or change your diet; you normally make more than one change at the same time. When you get the results you are seeking, you are in the dark as to what worked and what didn't from the changes you made, as you only see the cumulative effect.

You need to be able to identify exactly what works and what doesn't so that you can do more of what is working and stop doing what isn't working.

STEP 7

Pulling your plan together

You should now have at least one strategy identified for each key focus area of the Profit Accelerator Formula and have a plan for how you will approach each of them. You will also have clear and tangible targets set from Step 5 to aim for and have a clear timeframe by when the targets will be achieved.

STEP 8

Margin focus first – cost review

Your house needs to be in order first before targeting any additional volumes because if you aren't coping and making sufficient levels of profit now, then the situation may not necessarily improve with additional volumes – particularly if you are not delivering your products and services as efficiently and cost-effectively as possible.

Look at all of your overheads and identify ways to save money or restructure any processes so that they are done more efficiently. Negotiate better terms and prices with every supplier that you possibly can. Don't leave any stone unturned. Revisit the ideas in Chapter 10 for some added inspiration.

If you need to alter your prices, now is the time to make those changes before undertaking any of your new marketing activities or initiatives that encourage extra sales volume. The time spent will be worth it. You are preparing your 'Profit Rocket' for launch.

STEP 9

Take action

You may decide to focus on one area only or all four of the remaining areas. That is down to you, your confidence and how quickly you want to accelerate the growth of profits in your business. It is important that initially you limit yourself to one strategy per focus area, for the reasons indicated in Step 6.

STEP 10

Track everything and monitor it all closely

This really is key for the reasons that we have covered right throughout the book and especially in Chapter 5 when we covered setting targets. How do you know if something is improving or not unless you are tracking it? How do you know you have arrived at the destination unless you know where you intended to go and monitored your progress along the way?

Set up whatever systems are required to track and monitor your results. Get the help you need if you can't do it yourself.

So there you have it, a 10-step blueprint that you can use to help get you started, as I promised. Now, as we are reaching the closing stages of our time together, I think it is worth reflecting on some of the key messages we have covered.

Being in business isn't always easy. Don't be hard on yourself

Remember, if being in business were an easy thing to do then everyone would be doing it. We can sometimes be our own harshest critic. Go easy on yourself and take some time out regularly to reflect on the successes you have had and will have in the future. Celebrate those successes as you would celebrate the successes of others. Be kind to yourself.

It's okay to make mistakes

We are all human and we sometimes make mistakes. That's okay. In fact, some would argue that we are not truly living unless we make loads of mistakes. At least it means that we are trying new and unfamiliar things that push us out of our comfort zones. It's what we do when we make a mistake that sets us apart. If we learn from our mistakes and make improvements off the back of them, then that's called moving forward, but if we ignore the lessons and keep repeating the same mistakes then that's called stupidity.

Balance between 'working in' and 'working on' the business

An important but necessary distinction needs to be made between 'working in' and 'working on' a business. 'Working in' roughly translates to the 'doing part' of the business, i.e. the delivery of the products or services to your customers or clients, whereas 'working on' the business means focusing on activities and strategies to help move the business forward to its ultimate intended destination. You want to be 'working on' the business as much as possible and employing other resources where possible to do the 'working in' bit.

Numbers aren't scary

Numbers aren't scary mythical monsters; they can't hurt you physically but they do have tremendous power when harnessed properly. The numbers side of a business is one of the most important elements of any successful business venture, and if ignored it is important to recognise and acknowledge that there will be consequences.

Just like when you first learned to ride a bike, you didn't know how to do it. At the time, it was a foreign concept to you but you knew that you wanted to learn how to do it and were determined to do so. There is no difference between that experience and learning more about the numbers side of your business. It all comes down to your desire and willingness to take action.

You need to start somewhere and get help from the many resources available to take you through the training wheel stage through to the confident bike rider stage. We can't expect to be good at something instantly, and as with any new skill we need to practice and practice some more. That is the only way we will get better at something.

Remember the whole numbers side of your business is a skill set that can be learned, just like any other skill, and there's absolutely nothing to be scared about or any excuses whatsoever for not doing so.

Confronting money 'head trash'

We all have a belief system that is individual and unique to us. It shapes our take on the world and all the various components that make it up. Our belief system is a collection of thoughts and ideas that we believe to be true which have been accumulated through what we have been told, taught and experienced during our lives.

Remember, some of our beliefs work for us and some against us. The game is to encourage the development of behaviours and attitudes in terms of mind set and beliefs that work for us and to tackle and overcome those that work against us. It is being aware of what currently limits us and forms potential obstacles to our desired success that's important.

It's all about having a greater awareness of you. That means being aware of your tendencies to react in a certain way when it comes to money. Faced with this awareness, it then becomes a choice for you at that point. You are in a position to be making an informed response on how to balance your behaviour and likely reaction accordingly. Remember, evolution not revolution. Rome wasn't built in a day.

Marketing is an investment

The exact same principles that apply to investing apply to marketing. You need to have a balanced portfolio of marketing activities within your business so that you are not reliant on just one marketing activity. You need to know what is working and what isn't by constantly monitoring the results by testing and measuring them.

You want to stop the marketing activities that aren't working and do more of the marketing activities that are working. People and markets evolve, so something that is working one month may not necessarily work as effectively in another month. Having a portfolio of things that you do helps balance out this impact.

The distinction between conscious marketing and unconscious marketing is important. Conscious marketing is deliberate targeted marketing and should be seen as an investment. Like any investment, we expect to receive a return on our investment that is acceptable to us. Unconscious marketing that is not deliberate, not targeted and not measured is actually a cost to your business and should be stopped immediately.

Small improvements can lead to dramatic results

You were introduced to the Profit Accelerator Formula and I shared with you many ideas to help stimulate your thinking about each of the five key focus areas which are: number of leads, conversion rate, number of transactions, average sale value and margins.

I covered this area in a lot of detail so won't go over the same ground again. The important message for you is that small improvements in the specific key focus areas I shared with you can absolutely transform the level of profits your business is generating. The attention and power is in focusing on the right detail.

I have demonstrated to you how many small achievable changes to these areas can double or triple your profits and provided you with a 10-step blueprint for helping you to move forward and put what you have learned into action. Now that's something you should be very excited about!

Speed versus velocity

I want you to think about the distinction between speed and velocity for a moment. What do both words mean? What is the difference between their meanings?

Sure, both are related to how fast something is moving but there is a subtle yet important difference that is very relevant to the choices you make every day in your business.

Speed is defined as 'how fast something is moving', whilst velocity is defined as 'how fast something is moving in a given direction'. Let's think about what this really means. Take a hamster wheel for instance, what does the hamster typically do? A hamster runs like crazy as the wheel turns, gets worn out in the process and stops because it can't go on any longer.

My question to you is, having exerted all that energy, has that hamster actually gone anywhere? The answer is 'no'; it is still at exactly the same point as it was when it started, despite running like crazy as the wheel turned. The hamster has moved with speed, no doubt, but got nowhere despite all its efforts, as it is still physically in the same spot. It could try to run faster or could slow down if it chose. In either case it wouldn't matter, because it would still remain in that same spot irrespective of the speed at which it moves.

It's time to be completely honest with yourself. Are you, or do you sometimes feel like, that proverbial hamster stuck in a hamster wheel? Is it symbolic of your business, running like crazy by being busy doing things but not actually moving forward? Are you effectively treading water and growing wearier and more tired the longer you do it for? Could not the same energy you are using in the wheel be transferred to activities that represent 'velocity'? This means refocusing your energies and attention to activities that move your business forward. That is what velocity is all about. It's about speed in a specific direction.

Every day you choose to focus your energies on things that support your business moving forward and those that cause it to stand still. The more you focus your energies on activities that move your business forward, the greater velocity you will achieve. There is a subtle but important difference here, which I hope you can see.

So we reach the end of our journey together. You now find yourself right at that very intersection I described earlier in the book. You have to make a choice. There are only two paths in front of you. On the signpost in front of you, the one pointing left reads 'doing what you've always done' and the other, 'evolution not revolution'. The first path represents your choice to continue making excuses for not embracing the numbers side of your business. It represents doing what you have always done and getting the same results, good or bad.

The difference between these two paths is represented by the distinction between speed and velocity. The path to the left is the choice to be that proverbial hamster running like crazy in its little wheel but actually getting nowhere, because what you don't know at this point as you look up at the signpost is that this path is circular and may eventually lead you back to this very intersection. I say 'may' because there is no guarantee that your business will survive if the financial side continues to be neglected during the time it takes to navigate the path and come full circle.

The other path, to your right, involves you seeking help and having the real desire to improve your understanding on the numbers front and increasing your profits. It's about recognising your current limitations and doing something positive about it. It represents uncharted territory for you at this point, but you know that you have done things in the past that you didn't know how to do at the outset. You soon learned though, and became better and better at it as you practised your new skill and your confidence grew. Much like when you learned how to ride a bike, to swim or ride a horse. This is the path that represents velocity. It is using the same energy but focusing it on activities that keep your business moving in a forward direction.

Now, let's not dress it up to be anything it's not. You are faced with having to choose between continuing to make excuses or facing up to the challenge head-on and moving forward from here. I can't make that decision for you, nobody else can make that decision. You must make a decision, though. So what will it be – speed or velocity? Doing what you have always done and risking losing your business or taking your head out of the sand and embracing the numbers side of your business to make more profit today?

About the author

Kelly is a qualified accountant with over twelve years' working experience, predominantly in the UK, with the latter years at Finance Director level. His experience extends across industries and businesses of varying sizes – ranging from smaller enterprises through to the £3 billion fund of a listed company.

Kelly is really passionate about helping small business owners and entrepreneurs be as profitable as they can be, so he has taken all of the experiences and the things he has learned throughout his career to date to write this guide. He resigned by choice from his well-paid job as a Finance Director – in the middle of arguably the worst recession in living memory – to set up his company Profit in Focus so he can provide the vital tools, insights and resources that business owners need to transform the profits of their business.

Profit in Focus is a real, honest and genuine reflection of his open attitude to business, which is one of professional integrity, commitment and always seeking out opportunities for mutual benefit.

Kelly is known for helping small businesses to accelerate their profit growth rapidly and his mission is to leave his clients and the people he helps feeling invincible.

Connect with Kelly:

Linked In: http://www.linkedin.com/in/kellymclifford
Twitter: @profitinfocus
Website: http://www.profitinfocus.com
Find him on Google+

Resource Toolkit

Introducing the **Profit in Focus Foundation Toolkit**

Back in Chapter 3, I mentioned a toolkit that I have created specifically to help you understand more about the seven common mistakes that we covered in that chapter and to help prevent you from making the same mistakes yourself. The *Profit in Focus Foundation Toolkit* will help support you with this area and is designed to address the issues raised in the chapter.

This comprehensive toolkit contains seven modules:

- Understanding Your Balance Sheet
- Understanding Your Profit and Loss Statement
- Managing Your Cash Flow
- Profitable Pricing
- Breakeven Analysis
- Business Planning
- Budgets

Each module is supported by video content and includes a comprehensive workbook with case studies, worked solutions and a CD of various tools and templates to help you in your business. This toolkit enables you to learn and understand these areas from the comfort of your own home or office without fear of feeling embarrassed or being judged by others. It's a resource you can refer to time and time again.

SPECIAL READER OFFER

To say thank you for reading my book and to provide you with a real incentive to keep up the forward moving momentum, I am offering you as a valued reader a 15% discount when purchasing the **Profit in Focus Foundation Toolkit.**

Simply visit http://www.profitrocketbook.com for further details and enter the promotion code READER15 at checkout to claim your savings.

Help spread the word

If you have enjoyed reading the book, then please tell others about it. More details on how you can spread the word are on the book website so be sure to check out how you can help to do this. You will also find on the website further details of other products and services that **Profit in Focus** can help you with.

Enjoy!

Lightning Source UK Ltd.
Milton Keynes UK
UKOW040343030712

195373UK00002BA/4/P